Faculty of Color Navigating Higher Education

Faculty of Color Navigating Higher Education

Edited by
Karen Harris Brown,
Patricia Alvarez McHatton, and
Michelle Frazier Trotman Scott

ROWMAN & LITTLEFIELD
Lanham • Boulder • New York • London

Published by Rowman & Littlefield
A wholly owned subsidiary of The Rowman & Littlefield Publishing Group, Inc.
4501 Forbes Boulevard, Suite 200, Lanham, Maryland 20706
www.rowman.com

Unit A, Whitacre Mews, 26-34 Stannary Street, London SE11 4AB

British Library Cataloguing in Publication Information Available

Library of Congress Cataloging-in-Publication Data is Available

ISBN 978-1-4758-2350-9 (cloth: alk. paper)
ISBN 978-1-4758-2352-3 (electronic)

∞™ The paper used in this publication meets the minimum requirements of American
National Standard for Information Sciences—Permanence of Paper for Printed Library
Materials, ANSI/NISO Z39.48-1992.

Printed in the United States of America

Contents

Foreword

Michael Hester

For the last 10 years, I have held an upper administrative position at a regional comprehensive university, one half of a two-decade career at an institution that is also my alma mater. Participating in administrative meetings where enrollment and employment trends were regularly discussed, I became aware of the gap in racial demographics that disturbed me. Institutional archives document that the Black student population had blossomed (from less than 18% when I graduated in 1993 to more than 35% now). Yet publicly accessible records from human resources revealed that the numbers of Black faculty and staff lagged far behind (less than 10% Black faculty, less than 13% Black staff). According to a university report on campus diversity, our Black student population meets the definition of "Black Serving non-HBCU," qualifying for federal funding under Title III of the Higher Education Act of 1965, yet less than 40 of its more than 450 faculty members are Black.

While always supportive of diversity along a variety of axes (age, gender, race, religion, sexual affinity, etc.), the details of this particular situation—large numbers of Black students and small numbers of Black employees—focused my attention on the specific issue of Black faculty. Why did this disparity exist, and what could be done to address it? These questions spurred me to start a campuswide conversation with Black employees. And so in the spring of 2014, I contacted all Black employees at our university. That led to my communications with the editors of this book, and our actions together may help explain why I was chosen to provide an upper administrative perspective on the issue of faculty diversity.

Puzzled by the relative dearth of Black faculty and staff, I was determined to find answers to the questions that troubled me. How could our campus be so attractive to Black students, yet seemingly much less appealing to Black faculty and staff? What, if anything, should the university be doing to recruit and retain Black faculty? Talking with my fellow employees was the best way to address these questions. I e-mailed every Black employee on campus, inviting them to come together to discuss experiences, share stories, and collectively address two intertwined questions: how can our university identify, recruit, hire, and retain qualified Black employees in greater numbers? And based on the experiences of those Black employees already working here, what improvements need to be made to ensure that they are satisfied with their workplace?

This origin of the Association of Black Faculty (ABF) and Association of Black Staff (ABS) at our university can be understood as a microcosm of the larger issues on which this book is focused: the recruitment and retention of faculty of color by predominantly White institutions (PWIs) for the betterment of the university and to the fulfillment of the needs of the faculty themselves. Recognizing the differential between the demographics of the student population and the faculty as an *imbalance* that warranted corrective actions meant being of a mind-set where *little details* like this one are even noticed. Contacting every Black employee on a campus required creative thinking with regard to how such individuals could be identified, but even more so, it required being willing to talk about sensitive subjects with many people to whom I was a complete stranger, taking the risk of offending the very individuals whom I sincerely wanted to help. And finally, if these conversations I hoped to facilitate were going to be productive, our discussions would ultimately lead to proposals for institutional reforms, which necessitated being aware of and prepared for the thorny consequences that arise from expectations for and resistance to such change.

I omitted a key detail of this story. I am a Caucasian, a heterosexual male, born and raised in this country—benefiting daily from all the privileges that come with these labels. After 20 years at the same institution, I had risen from instructor to dean of the Honors College. Having been a first-generation college student who grew up in racially integrated settings, which frequently had me in the position of a *minority* among larger numbers of African Americans in my schools or on my athletic teams, I had been aware of the institutional and individual racism faced by people of color, and issues of racial discrimination had always been important to me. Now finding myself in a position of power, I felt an obligation to effectively advocate on behalf of minority employees and enact changes intended to address the lack of diversity and inclusion among the ranks of both faculty and staff.

I remember the first meeting our campus leadership (vice presidents, deans, etc.) had with the new university president. It was a breakfast with approximately 30 people in the room. There was age diversity, gender diversity (e.g., the majority of our college deans are female), geographic diversity, and diversity of occupation (student affairs, academic affairs, business and finance, and advancement were all represented). Racial and ethnic diversity was sorely lacking, as there was only one person of color in the room (a male of South Asian descent), and no Black people or non-White Hispanics at all. The president asked each of us to introduce ourselves. A pattern was established of introducing which part of the university you represented and listing some of the recent accomplishments of your unit. When it came my time to speak, after more than half had already introduced themselves, I chose not to talk about the Honors College's accomplishments. Instead, after stating my name and title, I said, "This room is too White. A third of our student body is Black, yet there's not a single Black person among our leadership at this breakfast. All of our vice presidents are White, all but one of our deans are White. We only have two African American department chairs. Addressing this issue should be a priority." Our new president responded positively, noting that increasing diversity among upper administration and across campus was indeed an issue he would focus on. Three years later, the university has hired two women of color into vice president positions, while momentum builds for addressing the continued imbalance between the relative diversity of our student body and the faculty.

This anecdote illustrates two important points. First, a lack of accessibility by underrepresented groups requires that individuals who are not members of said groups advocate on behalf of those who are not present. When there are no upper administrators of color, there can be no statements made in meetings among upper administrators about a lack of authority figures of color unless someone else raises the issue. In other words, collaborators are required. This is not because people of color cannot articulate their own concerns or because someone else can "do it better," but because *no one can speak in spaces where he or she is not present*. Collaborating first requires being aware, having empathy, for the lived experiences of others. But it requires more than mere empathy. Without action, empathy is no different than apathy.

Second, one cannot allow the perfect to be the enemy of the good when trying to find "the right time" to discuss diversity or discrimination. As the more conventional comments made by others indicated, the opening breakfast with the new president is not usually thought of as the time to discuss "heavy" issues; I could have easily sent the president an e-mail or sought a private meeting with him. But by being willing to break convention and speak out in that forum, I not only communicated an important message to the president—leadership from across the entire campus heard it as well. Speaking out about the needs of underrepresented groups already working as faculty on campus or advocating for action to increase the diversity of faculty should not, and cannot, wait until one is asked specifically about it. Bringing up these subjects whenever conversations are taking place about the institutional mission, the overall quality of campus life, and the values of the university is not "going off topic"—they are at the very core of discussions about how to transform our school into the best university it can be.

It is crucial that those who benefit from the privileges of power exercise their influence for greater diversity, inclusion, and social justice in ways that those for whom injustice is *lived* (not merely theorized in the abstract) cannot—without risking their professional and academic lives (and in the worst cases, their physical safety). Accepting that responsibility and being a good partner in efforts to promote diversity and inclusion requires that those of us with privilege—our race, our gender, our class, our nationality, our age, and so on—learn to engage with individuals of underrepresented groups. We must become aware of and sensitive to the significant differences in our lived experiences. That means meeting with faculty of color on their terms, allowing them to lead the conversation, accepting that our ignorance should defer to their expertise on these matters. That process of educating ourselves never stops; thus our awareness is increased along the way, as we seek opportunities to speak out on issues faced by our colleagues whose minority status on our campus too often keeps them from the levers of power over which we more frequently have greater control. This book makes a significant contribution to that effort by providing an outlet from which faculty of color can share their lived experiences and ideas for change and their travails and triumphs.

This book is immeasurably valuable for people of color in higher education who can gain insights from similarly positioned others about the problems they face, but the messages contained within these chapters are just as important for those of us who have benefited from being in the majority, so that we can help challenge and change the status quo. Technically, I occupy the position of the privileged administrator, who too often is the hindrance to positive change in stories of frustrated faculty of color. Just as my conversations with faculty of color at my institution helped me understand both the obstacles they face and potential solutions for overcoming these impediments, the experiences shared in this book can educate the "White males in charge" (and others), providing advice on how to stop being a barrier to and start becoming a positive force for productive change to improve the workplace satisfaction for faculty of color and increase their overall numbers on campus. In addition, it may offer all readers a few new ideas on how to successfully address the issues facing faculty of color that hamper not only promotion and tenure but also more enriching diversity and inclusion on campus.

Many PWIs across the country are in the process of addressing their lack of diversity and are attempting to create a more inclusive campus environment. Innovative ideas are being discussed using nearly every channel of communication in higher education. Individuals who share the common goal of promoting diversity and inclusion have ample opportunities to converse with one another about best practices. We must remember that talking about these issues may not always feel inspiring. Comprehending the full extent of the factors that are working against faculty of color may be so discouraging that trying to change the status quo feels like a waste of time. Success has to be measured in increments—positive changes in workplace satisfaction for a single faculty of color are meaningful. Even slight improvements in fostering a more welcoming campus atmosphere for faculty of color are worthwhile. Most important, the voices of faculty of color must be the guidepost every step of the way.

Conversations with members of the ABF at my university revealed heartbreaking stories from individuals whose career arcs had been distorted by racism—sometimes egregiously intentional and sometimes subtle and banal, but always maddening in its harmful effects on both the victims of the transgressions and the university that had been prevented from achieving its potential. Positive developments have been achieved for some members of the ABF and ABS, and progress has been made in some areas for every member, yet frustration remains for members with situations that have not improved enough or at all. However, independently of its influence on university policy, the ABF and ABS have also provided Black employees with a source of reassuring strength in numbers. During the first meeting, the expressions on the faces of the Black employees, as they looked around the room at the dozens of colleagues and realized that for the first time they were in a campus meeting in which *they were the majority*, told me my instincts had been right and well worth the effort. The collection of authors in this volume may similarly provide comfort to the reader that, indeed, there are others traveling the same road as the reader, an uplifting reminder that he or she is not experiencing this journey alone.

My own experience has revealed to me no magic potions, no money-back guarantees, and no silver bullets; determination and perseverance are required, while hope and optimism are recommended. The bonds created with those with whom you work toward a common cause may end up being the most memorable outcome of your efforts. In other words, our progress toward greater diversity and inclusion in higher education is very similar to the path we ask our students to take on their matriculation toward their academic degree—pride in the daily efforts and satisfaction when we achieve our goals, even as we realize how much work remains to be done.

BIBLIOGRAPHY

Li, X., & Carroll, C. D. (November 2007). *Characteristics of minority-serving institutions and minority undergraduates enrolled in these institutions: Postsecondary education descriptive analysis report. Institute of Education Sciences*. Washington,

DC: US Department of Education, Institute of Education Sciences, National Center for Education Statistics.

Presidential Committee on Campus Inclusion White Papers, Faculty and Student Sub-Committee Reports. Rep. N.P.: University of West Georgia, 2015. Print.

U.S. Census Bureau. *State & county quick facts*. Retrieved from http://quickfacts.census.gov/qfd/states/13/1304000.html, July 2015

UWG fact book. University of West Georgia, 2015. Retrieved from www.westga.edu/assetsDept/irp/Fact_Book__7.10.14.1.pdf

Preface

This book is the result of countless conversations with colleagues and other faculty of color across the nation about our experiences of working at predominantly White institutions. The stories revealed shared experiences within the academy that highlighted trials and triumphs as we negotiated the tenure and promotion process, addressed student resistance, and strived to become part of the fabric of the institution. We came to recognize the importance of telling our stories as a means of helping others who may benefit from realizing they are not alone and who may find within this text a sense of kinship and a renowned sense of agency.

Acknowledgments

We are grateful to Rowman & Littlefield, particularly Susanne Canavan, acquisitions editor—education, for the incredible support and guidance you provided. Thank you for agreeing to take on this project. For the contributing faculty authors who boldly shared their stories, we are in deep gratitude. Without your contributions, this book would not have been possible. We dedicate this book to the faculty members of color who were unable to share—due to hurtful memories and fear. May you find solace in the personal narratives.

Karen Harris Brown, Patricia Alvarez McHatton,
and Michelle Frazier Trotman Scott

Chapter 1

Faculty of Color in Higher Education

Karen Harris Brown, Patricia Alvarez McHatton, and Michelle Frazier Trotman Scott

> There is no greater agony than bearing an untold story inside of you.
>
> Dr. Maya Angelou (2014)

According to Kena et al. (2015), there were 1.5 million faculty (i.e., professors, associate professors, assistant professors, instructors, lecturers, assisting professors, adjunct professors, and interim professors) in degree-granting postsecondary institutions in fall 2013, of which 51 percent were full-time faculty members. Faculty of color represented less than half (approximately 21%) of all full-time faculty members during this time. Asians and Pacific Islanders constituted the largest percentage of faculty members of color at 10 percent, while Blacks and Hispanics/Latin@ represented only 6 percent and 5 percent, respectively, of all full-time instructional faculty members. American Indians and Alaska Natives and two or more races constituted the smallest percentage at less than 1 percent. In contrast, 84 percent of all postsecondary full-time faculty members were White (54% males and 26% females).

Research in higher education has revealed that poor retention of faculty of color is related to job satisfaction, organizational climate, and professional fit (Fries-Britt, Rowan-Kenyon, Perna, Milem, & Howard, 2011; Turner, Gonzalez, & Wood, 2008). Faculty members of color are not as satisfied with their job roles and responsibilities as their White counterparts (Ponjuan, Gasman, Hirshman, & Esters, 2011), and they face subtle hostile or challenging work environments at a disproportionately higher rate (Evans & Chun, 2007; Gonzalez & Harris, 2014). Often, these subtle acts, referred to as microaggressions, are manifested when these faculties' competence is questioned, their scholarship is devalued, their race or ethnicity is used as the sole criterion for committee invitations or requests, and inappropriate comments are

1

made based on cultural assumptions about ethnic groups which faculty of color represent (Orelus, 2013; Sue et al., 2011).

As colleges attempt to recruit and retain faculty of color in their institutions, the cultural competence levels of search committee members, department chairpersons, deans, and other college or university administrators are critical. A culturally competent stance can influence policies and decisions that can foster an environment that embraces and affirms diverse perspectives, research agendas, and "ways of knowing" what faculty of color bring to an institution. A responsive environment in which faculty of color can both survive and thrive beyond the search process is a necessity, especially when retention is considered.

Faculty members who have earned tenure, and/or who are in tenure-track positions, at predominantly White institutions (PWIs) were invited to share their experiences as chapters in this book. All have shared their experiences as faculty of color at PWIs of higher education. Some have also shared how they coped with or handled struggles or defeats and successes in the workplace and the methods used by college or university administrators and colleagues to support and retain faculty of color. It is our hope that these stories can be used to help faculty begin to have conversations about the issues of recruitment, retention, and support of faculty members of color. In addition, we hope that the stories can be used to provide insight and understanding to the colleagues and administrators of faculty of color, which in turn will positively influence the levels and quality of support.

The contributing authors represent a wide variety of individuals who identify as being *of color*. Racial and ethnic backgrounds represented include Black, Asian, Hispanic/Latin@, and multiracial. In addition, the book provides gendered perspectives as it includes voices from both female and male faculty of color who are currently or were previously employed as tenured or tenure-track faculty at PWIs of higher education.

Narrative research methodology is used by researchers across disciplines. It takes multiple forms, and the data can be analyzed in a variety of ways (Daiute & Lightfoot, 2004). For the purposes of this text, the term *narrative* will serve as both the phenomenon and the method of study (Pinnegar & Daynes, 2006). Through narratives or personal stories, what Connelly and Clandinin (2006) define as "a portal through which a person enters the world and by which their experience of the world is interpreted and made personally meaningful" (p. 375), the reader is provided a glimpse of the lived experiences of faculty of color. An essential element of narrative research is verisimilitude or trustworthiness. The stories, as told, must resonate with the reader affording a "vicarious experience of being in the similar situation and thereby being able to understand the decisions made and the emotions felt by the participants" (Loh, 2013). As such, each author provides a vivid account of an event or collective life experiences as faculty of color in PWIs (Denzin, 1989).

While there are similar themes throughout each of the narratives, each author takes a different perspective. The collective experiences may resonate with other faculty of color as well as with their White colleagues and provide a venue for open discussion regarding the lived experiences of faculty of color in PWIs specifically and higher education in general. The stories shed light on actions that may ameliorate a sense of marginalization, ensure faculty of color are provided a place at the table, and assist with the identification of support systems that need to be in place and would benefit faculty of color as well as others as they progress through the somewhat murky tenure and promotion process.

In Chapter 2, "Limits of Acceptance: How Far Is Too Far?," Ramanathan leads the sharing of lived experiences. In this chapter, she analyzes her profile and experiences using Root's (2000, 2004) and Renne's (1996) theories of multicultural identities. She discusses her isolating experiences and what she perceives is a myopic view of her experiences and qualifications. Her passion is teaching research courses and mentoring doctoral students; however, she is assigned to teach multicultural courses by virtue of her nationality or ethnic identity and international experiences. While she likes teaching ESOL and definitely multicultural courses, she perceives that the administration at her institution is unable to see and use her strengths. She details her privilege from a prominent family in her place of birth and the very different reception she has received upon entering academia in the United States. Ramanathan's story moves from seeking approval to wear her native dress to assuming her racial identity at will.

In Chapter 3, "The Sword, the Shield, and Double-Consciousness: Notes on Reconciling and Negotiating the Black Male Scholar Identity," Glenn discusses how the pernicious meta-narrative about Black males' intellectual capacity and behavioral predilections has pathologized their differences and obscured their talents. With the meta-narrative, he explores the dynamics of this (un)conscious battle Black males must perfect in an attempt to legitimize their place in the academy. Within his narrative, Glenn highlights the added cognitive load that Black males in academia must contend with, having to deal with the usual concerns about tenure and promotion, as well as his Blackness and perceptions based on his entity as a Black male, compared to their White counterparts as they negotiate their journey toward tenure.

In Chapter 4, "Navigating Higher Education as an Asian Immigrant Female," An shares the challenges and possibilities she has encountered as a first-generation Asian immigrant woman in the U.S. academia. She traces her journey from her childhood growing up in South Korea to young adulthood as an international graduate student in the United States to her current status as a tenure-track assistant professor at a PWI in the South. She describes her experiences as a model minority, which in some ways makes her invisible within the academy. She also discusses how her academic discipline, social studies, further marginalizes her due to its standing within the K–12 accountability movement. As a content area that is not *tested*, it is viewed as less important or unnecessary in some ways. An discusses the challenges she faced when race within the academy is presented as a dichotomy of Black and White, failing to take into account the lived experiences of other faculty of color with disparate histories that nonetheless lead to similar outcomes.

In Chapter 5, "The Silencing of International Faculty: The Enemy Inside and Out," Guerra describes a newly found awareness of the similarities of her experiences with that of other international faculty. It was not until she arrived in the United States that she recognized her identity as a Latina. In this new space, it became necessary to reconceptualize her identity in response to what she was experiencing. In her narrative, she takes a critical reflexive stance as she highlights how in addition to being silenced by the dominant group she has silenced herself in her struggle for survival in White-dominated academia. Like An, she too acknowledges the dichotomy of race within the academy and calls for unity as a means of improving outcomes for all faculty of color.

In Chapter 6, "Reframing Resistance: Steering into and through Student Resistance to Diversity Course Content," Smith shares a narrative describing his journey to reconcile persistent student resistance with an ever-evolving professional identity. He discusses how, as a faculty member of color, it feels increasingly vital to cultivate an active awareness and cache of strategies allowing him to recognize moments that require him to maneuver into, through, and around student resistance while staying intact personally, psychologically, and philosophically.

In Chapter 7, "A Lighthouse on the Shore, the Challenge of Trying to Shine," Thomas uses the metaphor of a lighthouse to describe her experiences in academia. With boldness she details the events surrounding the choice to self-advocate and the price she pays for doing this in the confines of a PWI. Facing a devastating loss, Thomas ends her narrative with specific steps that she believes would enable her and others to rebuild and move on.

In Chapter 8, "The Golden Child," our final narrative, Johnson provides a different perspective on experiences of faculty of color in PWIs. Her story is one of privilege in which she has benefited from the institution's attempt to diversify its faculty. She discusses the preferential treatment and extensive support she received during her tenure at a small PWI in the Southeast, while also being witness to disparate treatment of other faculty of color.

Chapter 9, "Thematic Analysis," is a summary of the collective experiences of authors. This summary is based on a thematic analysis of the narratives. As noted previously, there are some consistent themes within each of the narratives as well as distinct differences. The historical context within which each author exists, as well as the individual context of the institution in which he or she resides, is an important consideration in making the meaning of their experiences. Several significant findings emerged from the narratives. They had to reconceptualize their identity in light of their experiences. They revealed resiliency and responses that may be considered passive but are more demonstrative of purposeful behaviors based on contexts.

In Chapter 10, "Faculty of Color Navigating Higher Education," the final chapter, the editors have aligned themes discussed in Chapter 9 with recommendations and actions as a way of informing administrators and faculty of efforts that can support faculty of color. Using these findings, the editors discuss strategies, at both the individual and institutional levels, to ensure success for faculty of color as they move through the tenure and promotion process and attempt to navigate the political and racial climate encountered at these PWIs.

REFERENCES

Angelou, M. (2014). *Rainbow in the cloud: The wisdom and spirit of Maya Angelou.* (p. 47). New York, NY: Random House, LLC.

Connelly, F. M., & Clandinin, D. J. (2006). Narrative inquiry. In J. Green, G. Camilli, & P. Elmore (Eds.), *Handbook of complementary methods in education research* (pp. 375–385). Mahwah, NJ: Lawrence Erlbaum.

Daiute, C., & Lightfoot, C. (Eds.) (2004). *Narrative analysis: Studying the development of individuals in society.* Thousand Oaks, CA: Sage.

Denzin, N. K. (1989). *Interpretive biography.* Newbury Park, CA: Sage.

Evans, A., & Chun, E. (2007). Coping with behavioral and organizational barriers to diversity in the workplace. CUPA-HR Journal, Vol. 58, No. 1, 12–18.

Fries-Britt, S. L., Rowan-Kenyon, H. T., Perna, L. W., Milem, J. F., & Howard, D. G. (2011). Underrepresentation in the academy and the institutional climate for faculty diversity. *Journal of the Professoriate, 5*(1), 1.

Gonzalez, C. G., & Harris, A. P. (2014). Presumed incompetent: Continuing the conversation. *Berkeley Journal of Gender, Law & Justice, 29,* 183–195. Retrieved from http://scholarship.law.berkeley.edu/bglj/vol29/iss2/1

Kena, G., Musu-Gillette, L., Robinson, J., Wang, X., Rathbun, A., Zhang, J., . . ., Dunlop, V. E. (2015). *The condition of education 2015 (NCES 2015–144).* Washington, DC: U.S. Department of Education, National Center for Education Statistics. Retrieved from http://nces.ed.gov/pubs2015/2015144.pdf

Loh, J. (2013). Inquiry into issues of trustworthiness and quality in narrative studies: A perspective. *The Qualitative Report, 18,* article 65, 1–15. Retrieved from http://www.nova.edu/ssss/QR/QR18/loh65.pdf

Orelus, P. W. (2013). The institutional cost of being a professor of color: Unveiling micro-aggression, racial [in]visibility, and racial profiling through the lens of critical race theory. *Current Issues in Education, 16*(2), 1–11. Retrieved from http://cie.asu.edu/ojs/index.php/cieatasu/article/viewFile/1001/485

Pinnegar, S., & Daynes, J. G. (2006). Locating narrative inquiry historically: Thematics in the turn to narrative. In D. J. Clandinin (Ed.), *Handbook of narrative inquiry: Mapping a methodology* (pp. 3–34). Thousand Oaks, CA: Sage.

Ponjuan, L., Gasman, M., Hirshman, E., & Ester, L. (2011). A New Hope: Recruiting and Retaining the Next Generation of Faculty of Color. Association of Public and Land Grant Research Universities (APLU).

Renn, K. A. (2000). Patterns of situational identity among biracial and multiracial college students. *Review of Higher Education, 23*, 399–420.

Renn, K. A. (2004). Mixed race students in college: The ecology of race, identity, and community. Albany, NY: SUNY Press.

Root, M. P. P. (1996). *Multiracial experience: Racial borders as a new frontier.* Thousand Oaks, CA: Sage.

Sue, D. W., Rivera, D. P., Watkins, N. L., Kim, R. H., Kim, S., & Williams, C. D. (2011). Racial dialogues: Challenges faculty of color face in the classroom. *Cultural Diversity and Ethnic Minority Psychology, 17*(3), 331–340.

Turner, C. S. V., Gonzalez, J. C., and Wood, J. L. "Faculty of Color in academe: What 20 years of literature tells us." Journal of Diversity in Higher Education 1, no. 3 (2008): 139–168.

Chapter 2

Limits of Acceptance

How Far Is Too Far?

Hema Ramanathan

I have many identities: a faculty of color; a faculty with an international affiliation; a faculty whose teaching and research interests are in ethnic, particularly language, diversity. Each of these individually can contribute to an isolating experience. All together, they guarantee that the administrations at my institutions are unable to access my strengths.

Five critical incidents are described and examined to show how they have shaped my perception of myself as a faculty of color. The confluence of personal and institutional factors is analyzed using Root's (1996) and Renn's (2000, 2004) theories of multicultural identities. I identify the level of scale in which I situate myself for each facet of my multiple identities. In addition, I provide examples of development at each level.

MY ETHNIC EVOLUTION

A Citizen of the World

Like most Indian Americans who emigrate to the United States, I have an enormous amount of academic and social capital. I come from a family that values education, is involved in the arts, and was supportive of my desire to study in the United States. Living in a joint family reinforced the extended family unit as an integral value. Growing up with servants at home provided a second-hand experience of poverty, more than faintly paternalistic, but inculcated consideration for those less fortunate than I.

While my family members were Hindus, I experienced religious diversity studying in a missionary school. I learned the mythologies and religious texts of both Catholicism and Hinduism. This made me accept both as philosophies but left me uninterested in practicing either, making me an agnostic in my teens, which my family accepted unquestioningly.

Growing up, we were bilingual (Tamil and English) at home and I studied two additional languages (Hindi and Sanskrit) for a total of three different scripts—Latin (English), Grantha (Tamil), and Devanagri (Hindi and Sanskrit). I retain conversational fluency in these three; Sanskrit is not a commonly spoken language. Multilingualism also featured in my cultural experiences; I learned classical music with songs in three languages and regularly watched movies (without subtitles) in Hindi, Tamil, and English.

I had two opportunities to explore my identity and ethnicity before I came to the United States. I lived and worked in Indonesia, where I was for the first time conscious of being an Indian. I was the only South Asian person on the faculty of the English language school; the others were Indonesians or Caucasians. I was also the only vegetarian.

In Malaysia, I taught at an international school. The fairly even split of Chinese–Koreans and Europeans–South Americans with a few South Asians thrown in ensured a rich mix of races and ethnicities among the students. The faculty was an even split of Europeans and Indians. Though I was an Indian by ethnicity, I was hired on an expatriate contract for legal purposes. I thus had my feet in both camps. I was invited to cricket matches and parties hosted by the White community and to the ethnic festivals celebrated by the Indians.

I learned to adjust to the cultural norms and expectations of the dominant community of the country and the group with which I socialized. I was comfortable with being the interpreter of cultures. I was called upon to be an interlocutor to both "natives" and expatriates and the third viewpoint in an argument about culture. This level of comfort seemed to warrant a warning that I was in a danger of "falling between two stools" and losing my Indian identity.

When I moved to the United States for my doctoral studies, I brought with me the sense and awareness of privilege, both as a member of the dominant group and as a racial and ethnic minority.

Faculty at Predominantly White Institutions

Like many Indian American scholars, I came to the United States over two decades ago for graduate studies. Again, like many of them, I stayed on to teach, first in a private university in the Midwest (U-MW) and later in a Tier II institution in a university in the South (U-S), both of which are predominantly White institutions (PWIs).

At U-MW, I initially taught pedagogy and methods courses, and my research and professional commitment was in teacher education. I was also assigned to teach another course on multicultural education in the graduate program. As the only minority in the college, albeit without theoretical or academic background in multicultural education and diversity, I was deemed to have personal experience that would enrich student experiences and knowledge. Similarly, when my lobbying efforts for adding courses about English language learners (ELLs) in the teacher education programs were successful, the experiences of having taught English in three different countries in Asia as well as my degrees in Teaching English as a Second Language (TESOL) were deemed sufficient qualifications for me to teach the course.

During the promotion and tenure process, since at that point I was teaching only teacher education–related courses, I was encouraged and supported to present at conferences focusing on teacher education rather than ELLs. Since the TESOL association's affiliate in my state was not very active at that time, I drew on the special interest groups of teacher education–focused professional associations such as the Association of Teacher Educators and the American Educational Research Association to learn and be informed about ELLs and ESOL in the United States. Joining TESOL International Association eventually after I was tenured was at my own expense of time and money.

At U-S, my teaching responsibilities were primarily in the ESOL program where we offered an endorsement and on pedagogy in the doctoral program. When an opportunity arose after a few years, I began teaching courses on diversity in both the undergraduate and doctoral programs, again by virtue of my research interest in language diversity.

A PROFUSION OF LENSES

About halfway through the first quarter of my doctoral program, I sought an interview with the chair of the program and expressed my feelings of inadequacy and inability to cope with the expected academic rigor. I was no "spring chicken" and had not been a student for a long time. The professor's analysis of my "problem" was my first encounter with multiculturalism in the United States: I was processing all the information through the lens of three different educational systems—India, Indonesia, and the United States, the first two owing to my personal experiences and the third because of the setting for discussion in the course. For instance, in Indonesia, teachers were expected to encourage the students to attend the Saturday morning session focused on national integration, a practice not common in India while the U.S. focus on individuality ran counter to this cultural value. Trying to unravel the political and societal forces that engendered these vastly different behaviors was an exercise in "information overload" for a graduate student. While this may have enriched classroom discussions, it was no surprise I was overwhelmed. The chair of the program suggested that in addition to the

United States, which would be essential for an understanding of the prescribed readings, I should select one of the two other countries for continued discussion in the course, preferably India because I knew it more intimately than Indonesia. The strategy to "funnel" my ideas stood me in good stead during my dissertation, but more importantly this was one of the few occasions on which my non-mainstream experience was valued and validated in academia.

As a graduate student, I was also very fortunate to be one of 10 teaching assistants, five international students from around the world and five U.S. nationals, who were all European Americans, a mindful decision by the director of the program. The different perspectives that we brought to our teaching and our discussion in the faculty room further made me comfortable with having perceptions that were not mainstream American. Sadly, my experiences as a faculty have not been as supportive of my international/minority status as my graduate program was.

A MATTER OF APPEARANCE

In my first appointment as faculty, as a junior faculty at U-MW, I was focused on fitting in, not on challenging the essence of ethnic identity. As is apparent in Figure 2.1 based on the concepts defined by Hall (1976), appearance is in the visible 10 percent of the cultural iceberg, and anxious to be accepted as a professional, I dressed decorously in Western dresses. I tried to hold a monoracial identity (Renn, 2004) and to identify with a single racial dominant group (Root, 1996).

At the end of that year, believing I had established myself adequately through faculty interactions and positive student evaluations, I felt confident enough to think about making changes. When I hesitantly approached the dean and senior faculty about wearing Indian rather than Western clothes, I was given permission to dress in what would be considered formal wear in India. Since then I have always dressed in "ethnic clothes," though to me they are as normal as skirts and pants are to American peers.

This incident highlighted for me how dependent I am on the judgment of others. I needed to get permission to look different, and that had to be sanctioned by the administration and the dominant group. Now as a senior faculty who has gained tenure at two institutions, I choose not to pander to others' perceptions of what is considered professional attire and continue to wear Indian clothes to conferences and interviews. My appearance is a statement that apparel other than skirts and dresses can be professional, more than "fancy clothing" to be relegated to special days celebrating international day.

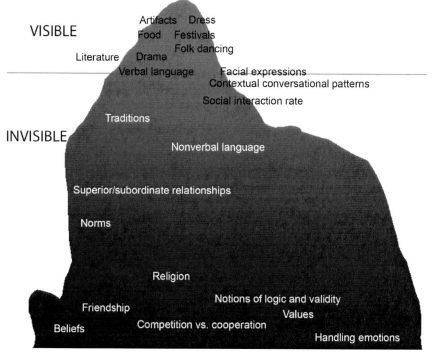

Figure 2.1. Iceberg Model of Culture. Adapted from *Beyond Culture* (1976) by Edward T. Hall.

My ethnic dress is also a political statement about the institution's claim to accepting and celebrating diversity, daring it to "walk the talk." As I go into schools in rural Georgia dressed in Indian clothes, I represent United States' acceptance of diversity.

Most K–12 teachers who see me either are accepting of me as I am dressed or may be too polite to question the professionalism of my appearance. However, professors are not immune from societal stereotypes that link physical appearance to assumptions about cultural backgrounds (Renn, 2004); a few K–12 teachers, meeting me for the first time as I walk into their classrooms to supervise my students in their field experiences, presume that I am unfamiliar with educational issues in the United States, such as requisite standards and testing processes, a misconception that I quickly and gently clarify.

Being considered "forever a foreigner" (Tuan, 1998) is not detrimental to my self-concept, but it is an ongoing struggle to ensure that I am not reacting to any stereotypes the dominant group may have of me because of my appearance. I do not cede the concept of professionalism to the dominant community in terms of dress. I retain the right to dress as I please, so long as it does not become too much of a distraction to learning. To tell all the truth but tell it slant (Dickinson, 1998), to give both students and teachers time to get accustomed to my appearance, for the first few meetings I dress in more muted "earth" colors and wear minimum jewelry, even toning down my signature large earrings.

LOOKING AND SEEING

The third instance will be familiar to many faculty of color. I was teaching a graduate course on diversity at U-MW, and all the students were European Americans, as was common in this PWI. In the first class meeting of this particular semester, after the preliminaries had been observed, my students were invited to ask me questions about myself, no holds barred. In the second half of the session, I asked them to describe me to a friend who had never met me. In the next 10 minutes, they listed many biographical details such as my educational qualifications and my teaching experiences, including the obvious fact that I was an instructor of this course; they commented on my proficiency in English and that I speak very clearly and am comprehensible, even if not with an American accent; they mentioned personal attributes such as a pleasant personality and kindness of manner. In these respects, there were no tensions about how I was expected to be and how I wanted to be perceived as a professional.

However, there were tensions in how I was expected to be and how I wanted to be perceived as an ethnic being (Chang & Kwan, 2009). The students did not mention my race, which is Asian Indian; my color, which is an unmistakable brown; nor that I am an immigrant. I was amused by their blatant disregard of the obvious. To elicit the detail of my race, I specifically asked them: If your friends were to come to the university and ask for me, what would be the most recognizable feature? On being questioned about their hesitancy in noting an apparent and obvious fact, they explained that they did not want to be impolite or to hurt or insult me.

I was irritated that they blithely overlooked all my unique experiences as an immigrant. While as teachers they touted the uniqueness of each student, attested to by the various posters around their schools, they were not willing to accord me the same appreciation. I was seriously disturbed by their response to the value-added perception of race and their lack of understanding of how color contributes to my persona. In this racialized society, they perceived being anything but White as a negative. They obviously did not subscribe to the positive model minority stereotype of Asian Americans but were placing a negative value on being brown. Instead, they were according me the honor of being an "honorary White." However, I ignored that omission.

After all, almost two decades ago, immigration was not as much a hot-button issue in education as it is now.

When lip service is paid to celebrating diversity, and appreciation is expressed in terms of sameness, it results in a racial status quo. In a PWI, the blandness of university culture could allow students to believe that all people should aim to be "us." This incident highlighted for me the urgent need to integrate antiracist pedagogy into cultural diversity coursework, so that students know and experience the differences that make up this diverse society and challenge their own beliefs and assumptions. The activities I have incorporated into my coursework (Ramanathan, 2010) are designed to make the students think and feel—to address the cognitive and affective domains. They focus on both linguistic and cultural understandings that students should acquire.

BORDER CROSSING

As a faculty member who is transnational and whose research interests span both the United States and India, I have a dual identity and am adept at "border crossing," being comfortable in both cultures professionally and personally. In fact, I frequently inhabit "no-man's-land," being between the two cultures. But balancing both identities as a teacher and a scholar is a delicate and exhausting exercise and often a thankless task.

At my interview at U-MW I was assured that my diverse experiences of teaching in three countries around the world—India, Indonesia, and Malaysia—were a major factor in my being hired. In an effort to play to this strength, I attempted to internationalize the curriculum in different ways. With the explicit support of the college and the university, I successfully placed a student teacher in a school in India that had been specifically trained to receive and supervise her according to the university's requirements. However, this experience was deemed unsuccessful on the basis of a European American administrator's impression of India, ostensibly on the basis that the Indian school did not align with U.S. state standards. Neither the student teacher's own statements nor my more intimate knowledge of the situation weighed against the administrator's condemnation of the program.

I was powerless in that situation. I had no one who could or would talk for me. I was not a part of either the conversations or the decisions that were made behind closed doors. That experience has made me wary of advancing an international agenda at the institutional level. Though I have deep, long-lasting relations with schools and communities in India, I have not been called on to build these bridges or cross these borders.

Even though I have learned to limit the international component to my own scholarship, the difficulties of establishing bona fides as a comparative education researcher have affected me negatively in the promotion process. Insisting on peer-reviewed journal articles as the sole criterion for the demonstration of scholarship and devaluing the importance of policy-related reports shows a lack of understanding of the issues of impact and accessibility in developing regions and promotion and tenure committees' lack of interest in and understanding of the target country's education agenda. For instance, South Asia does not yet have a significant culture of journals that are accessed by professionals, and decisions about education are primarily made by noneducationists. Therefore, publishing only in peer-reviewed journals is unlikely to have an impact on policy or in these regions. Further, journals are not always available online, and hard copy proofs of publications for tenure dossiers are not always available, due to prohibitive mailing costs and the unreliability of the postal systems. Thus, maintaining a balance between U.S.-based publications, which provide materials for faculty performance reviews, and other-country-focused scholarship fragments a research agenda to the detriment of scholars of comparative education.

A HOSTILE ENVIRONMENT

In some instances, the reason for discrimination is very clear, as in the earlier four instances where my minority status and international focus were the sources of disaccord and conflict. In other cases, perception may be reality, but it is difficult to objectively "prove" the provenance of discrimination to the satisfaction of those not affected by it, which, of course, is not a reason to discount the role and impact of racial and ethnic differences in engendering bias.

This final incident, a classic in Freirean terms of the oppressed finding the strength and means to educate and challenge the oppressor (Freire & Ramos, 2000), was one such case. My professional identity was assailed, but I could find no rational, "objective" explanation of why this should happen. By default, and by the "pricking of my thumbs," I attribute it to my racial and ethnic identity.

As a tenured senior faculty member with a solid record of teaching, scholarship, and service, it was a shock to my system when I found the environment in my college at U-S hostile, and I was at the receiving end of unfair, arbitrary, and capricious treatment that spanned a year. I was threatened with a professional growth plan and breaking of my tenure; summarily removed from two courses in the middle of the semester without due process; bullied and verbally abused at an official meeting; and not awarded promotion.

The first indication I had of this sustained effort to dislodge me from my position as a tenured faculty was when my past and present chairs called a meeting to put me on a professional growth plan, citing low student evaluations in one course I had taught the previous year. I was surprised since this matter had been dealt with in my annual performance review to the satisfaction of my then chair, and my evaluations otherwise were high. When I reminded them that the content was out of my area of expertise, that I had been given only 10 days to prepare for it, and that I was unlikely to teach this course again, I was asked to draft a memo to that effect in lieu of a professional growth plan. That this matter was not broached again once I had made it clear that I had dropped plans of going up for promotion seemed a coincidence that I brushed aside.

The following semester, when I was away at professional conferences that fell at the beginning of the term, I received an e-mail from the dean objecting to my absence at a collegewide meeting as a "nonappearance [that] could have been interpreted as abandonment of [my] contract." Given the prior approved travel authorization by my chair and two reminders to him in the previous week with assurances that my online classes were under way, this seemed not only uncalled for, but highly inappropriate. When I returned to campus, there were no references made to it even at a personal meeting with my chair and was no explanation or apology offered for these threats by any administrator.

The next event was being summarily reassigned from my classes midway through the semester. I was also informed at that time that I was still on the professional growth plan that I had never signed on to and I thought had been downgraded to a memo. There were no data provided and no paper trail was established to record student dissatisfaction so deep as to make personnel changes midterm. I was not allowed to talk to the students, and there was no opportunity to discuss the validity of these "complaints." There was no due process, nada, nil.

At a meeting to discuss this "lack of professionalism" on my part, I was bullied and verbally abused by my chair, who stated repeatedly that I was "not a good teacher" and that my scholarship was lacking. The dean and another chair sat by, silent spectators to this flagrant display of power, shocking behavior unheard of in academia. The outcome of the meeting was a project with unrealistic deadlines and unreasonable and demeaning working conditions. If I failed to meet these arbitrary requirements, I was threatened, in writing, with dismissal from the university, in spite of my tenured status.

I can find no justification for the behavior of my college administration. I had had extremely limited personal interactions with them, which, in my mind, was not sufficient to build up a personal animus. The only explanations offered were vague and unsatisfactory, including "personality clashes" and "a lack of communication," while not pinning responsibility on any one administrator.

As a faculty member of a nondominant group, I tried to resolve what I perceived as stereotypical and prejudicial treatment by the dominant White population that took aim at my professionalism and were direct assaults on my self-concept (Phinney, 1990). I had two choices: to fold my tent and steal away into the night—or to stay and fight this through. I chose the latter for two major reasons.

First, I found people were appalled by the treatment meted out to me and were willing to help me and work with me. They could be classified broadly into two categories: peer support group and university administrators. The peer support group included colleagues in academia inside and outside of my university, former students, personal friends, and my family. They performed three functions: cheerleader, touchstone, and headhunter. As cheerleader, they provided emotional support and contributed to keeping my faith in myself and shoring up my self-esteem. Using them as a touchstone, I sounded out ideas, seeking assurance that I was not misreading the situation and that my demands were legitimate and appropriate. As headhunters, they offered other options to me across the world so that I had choices and did not feel bound to stay on at the university in such trying conditions.

I reached out to university administrators across campus including the provost, the ombuds office, American Association of University Professors (AAUP) representatives, and deans of other colleges. I appealed to the university administration to enable me to continue to contribute professionally as a faculty member without being subject to stressful and demeaning actions. It took two successive provosts six months to give me relief, which took the form of moving me to another department, away from a chair who had bullied me, and encouraging me to apply for promotion the following year. Finding this support group who provided access to the corridors of power was crucial in my decision to continue at the university. The university administration was willing to listen to and support me, demonstrating to my satisfaction that my tenure was secure. A university committee on diversity was constituted. A series of seminars focused on diversity and discrimination provided a forum for identifying campuswide discriminatory practices and exploring constructive steps toward equity and fairness.

The second major reason for staying and fighting was a personal value I hold. I believe that as a faculty member with tenure I have a responsibility to speak up when I see injustice. Tenure gives me the security to point out discriminatory practices. It gives me the power to protect junior faculty who are not protected by tenure. Leaving the university at this juncture to suit my needs would have been a denial of a fundamental purpose of tenure.

I am aware that not all faculty will have the options that I do. Not everyone will be able or prepared to walk away from a home and a job and move at short notice. Nor can everyone cast the worldwide net as I was afforded due to my international research focus. However, it brought home to me the importance of keeping myself relevant even after tenure.

MOVING FORWARD

As an immigrant, I have filtered my ethnic identity through negative treatment received from others, questioning the value of my ethnicity, experiences, and selfhood at different points in my career. Sometimes it would have been easier for me to step back and become acculturated into the dominant culture, perhaps by adopting Western dress and basing my scholarship agenda solely in the United States. Amalgamating my ethnicity with my professionalism is difficult since there are few models and the literature on this topic is still in its infancy.

Multiple acculturation (Banks, 1994), the incorporation of different heritages into the identity development process, gives faculty of color strength and tensility to successfully meet all the challenges that face us. My international perspective, influenced by my considerable teaching experiences in three other countries, is an intrinsic part of my worldview, and it informs my teaching and my scholarship, for the betterment of my students, I am sure.

My early life in India afforded me "deep conscious immersion into cultural traditions and values through religious, familial, neighborhood, and educational communities, instill(ing) a positive sense of ethnic identity and confidence" (Chávez & Guido-DiBrito, 1999, p. 39). Border studies that examine the intersection of cultures and the resulting effects are a "significant frontier" (Root, 1996), a new territory for exploration—perhaps a new research agenda for me, informed by my recent experiences.

REFERENCES

Banks, J. (1994). *Multiethnic education: Theory and practice*. Boston, MA: Allyn and Bacon.

Chang, T., & Kwan, K. K. (2009). Asian American racial and ethnic identity. In N. Tewari & A. N. Alvarez (Eds.), *Asian American psychology: Current perspectives* (pp. 113–133). New York, NY: Taylor & Francis.

Chávez, A. F., & Guido-DiBrito, F. (1999). Racial and ethnic identity and development. In R. S. Caffarella and M. C. Clark (Eds). New directions for adult and continuing education: An update on adult development theory: New ways of thinking about life course (84, pp. 39–48). San Francisco, CA: Jossey-Bass.

Dickinson, E. (1998). Tell all the truth but tell it slant. In R. W. Franklin (Ed.), *The poems of Emily Dickinson: Reading edition*. New York, NY: The Belknap Press of Harvard University Press.

Freire, P., & Ramos, M. B. (2000). *Pedagogy of the oppressed.* New York, NY: Continuum International Publishing Group.

Hall, E. T. (1976). *Beyond cultures.* Garden City, N.Y.: Anchor Books.

Phinney, J. S. (1990). Ethnic identity in adolescents and adults: Review of the research. *Psychological Bulletin, 108,* 499–514.

Ramanathan, H. (2010). But they don't speak English: Mapping how we teach culturally and linguistically diverse learners. In U. Thomas (Ed.), *Culture or chaos in the village: The journey to cultural fluency.* Lanham, MD: Rowman & Littlefield.

Renn, K. A. (2000). Patterns of situational identity among biracial and multiracial college students. *Review of Higher Education, 23,* 399–420.

Renn, K. A. (2004). *Mixed race students in college: The ecology of race, identity, and community.* Albany, NY: SUNY Press.

Root, M. P. P. (1996). *Multiracial experience: Racial borders as a new frontier.* Thousand Oaks, CA: Sage.

Tuan, M. (1998). *Forever foreigners or honorary whites: The Asian American experience today.* New Brunswick, NJ: Rutgers University Press.

Chapter 3

The Sword, the Shield, and Double-Consciousness

Notes on Reconciling and Negotiating the Black Male Scholar Identity

Tristan L. Glenn

ON ACCESS AND OPPORTUNITY

It was the end of spring, and another school year was drawing to a close. My wife and I were attending a parent workshop for the Talented and Gifted Program (TAG) at our son Kingstan's school. He was completing the third grade and had been selected to participate in the gifted program for the following school year. Being selected to participate in the TAG program was something that Kingstan had been hoping for since the beginning of the school year, and as the parent workshop approached, he could barely contain his enthusiasm. Filled with excitement, which paled in comparison to our son's, we arrived at the conference with anticipation of what was to come.

The workshop went well. The TAG program teacher shared pertinent information that would be vital to the prospective students' success in the program. At the conclusion of the workshop, the teacher asked my wife and me to stay behind to talk further about our son. In the subsequent conversation, she revealed that, in spite of performing in the 90th percentile in the initial screening, Kingstan did not meet an additional requirement for placement in the program. Upon hearing this I was perplexed and naturally wanted to know more. What criteria had he failed to meet? The teacher explained that there was an additional classroom screening that teachers used to measure students on criteria such as motivation, interests, communication skills, problem-solving abilities, memory, inquiry, insight, reason, creativity, and humor. The goal of this measure was to identify students with superior abilities in five or more of these areas. Unfortunately, Kingstan's teacher did not initially rate him high enough in five of the areas. Thus, his *composite* score was not high enough for participation. Upon further consideration of his academic performance, the TAG teacher stated that she believed that he was an ideal candidate for the program, and, as a result, she went back to his homeroom teacher and asked her to consider rating him again. Ultimately, his homeroom teacher reevaluated him and Kingstan received higher area scores on the measure, thus, qualifying him to participate in the program.

We perceive the behaviors, choices, and actions of others based on both our direct and indirect interactions. When our direct interactions are limited, we often use the stories we receive about them as markers of their existence (Thomson, 1997). This practice frequently occurs despite its frequently inaccurate or false conclusions, and this is where the issue of misinterpretation and the subsequent costs are intensified. Due to its regularity, I believe this issue is worthy of deconstruction. Therefore, in this chapter I will explore issues of Black male identity focusing primarily on my experiences as a faculty of color at a primarily White institution (PWI) and unpack the importance of consciousness of the cultural meta-narrative that governs our thinking about *the other* and the ways it impacts our understanding of them.

In addition to a dialogue on perceptions of behavior, I will attempt to explicate issues of Black male identity. Focusing primarily on my experiences as a faculty of color at a PWI, I will make connections between my personal narrative and the broader social and cultural contexts of our society. Evidenced within my story will be the realization that I have experienced many of the issues of which I contend with in my current role as a faculty of color at differing levels and with varying degrees of significance throughout my life. Most of these experiences have required me to search for answers to resolve certain internal conflicts. Moreover, they have forced me to reconcile with the fact that certain things are simply an unfortunate consequence of my racial identity.

In divulging my narrative, I will share how these experiences have shaped my identity. But more important, I will provide insight into how I reconcile and negotiate my identity as a male Black intellectual operating in predominantly White spaces. Reaching into the origins of my personal history, I will attempt to contextualize the lens that personifies the bedrock of my conception of self and others. In this narrative, I provide a sincere discussion of my understanding of and resistance to the meta-narrative as well as the offensive and defensive techniques I exercise in this process. Specifically, I will expound on my applications of my metaphor of the sword and the shield in predominantly White spaces. I will end with a discussion of my concluding thoughts or questions as well as considerations for tenure and promotion as I respond to the expectations of that process.

I decided to begin my narrative with this vignette because I believe it serves as an appropriate departure point for the discourse presented in this chapter. This experience with my son highlights the (mis)perceptions of

Black male behavior and the potential costs levied on Black males when these misperceptions occur. In addition, I believe that if we are to somehow bring awareness to the harmful effects that result from the frequent (mis)perception of our behavior, we must speak candidly about how this dilemma impacts us all regardless of age, education level, or social status.

Misperceptions of behaviors happen on a daily basis. Our proficiency at displaying behaviors that exemplify norms of conduct often determines how our actions will be perceived. Equally, our confirmation to established behavior norms influences the degree to which we have access to opportunities, power, and privilege. In Kingstan's case, he proficiently demonstrated acceptably atypical academic aptitude. That is, his atypical demonstrations of knowledge were valued in this context. However, according to his teacher's initial assessment, he did not proficiently display other behaviors deemed as valuable according to the contextual criteria. For me, the fact that his teacher's first classroom screening revealed that he had fallen short of the canon was perplexing. I was mystified because in spite of his clear evidence of exceptional intellectual aptitude (which should indicate his superiority in at least five of the criteria), she did not recognize him as being capable. After further consideration of the 10 criteria, I was sure that her evaluation of him was a clear misperception of his behavior, a belief that I based on the fact that I witnessed him display behaviors such as motivation, interests, communication skills, problem-solving abilities, memory, inquiry, insight, reason, creativity, and humor at superior levels in both formal and informal settings. Moreover, there I knew that a strong correlation existed between the aforementioned skills and those evaluated in the academic aptitude assessment. At any rate, his potential for success in the TAG program was overlooked as his behavior was misperceived.

NASCENT NEGOTIATIONS OF RACIAL IDENTITY

> Conditions of life tied to identity . . . still mystify me. But now I have a working idea about where they [derive]. They come from the way a society, at a given time, is organized around an identity like race. That organization reflects the history of a place, as well as the ongoing individual and group competition for opportunity and the good life. (Steele, 2010, p. 3)

Beverly Tatum (1997) asserted, "The aspect of identity that is the target of others' attention, and subsequently of our own, often is that which sets us apart as exceptional or 'other' in their eyes" (p. 21). In my life, the most salient aspect of identity that has set me apart as *other* has been my race. That said, to contextualize my narrative, I believe it is necessary for me to reflect on my earliest experiences with race and how I initially came to understand my own.

As I reflected on my past experiences, I could not recall obvious moments in which race played a prominent role in my existence. I believe this was a result of the protection provided by my mother as well as the environment in which I lived. For the majority of my childhood, the people with whom I lived, played, worshipped, and studied were Black. In fact, excluding my teachers and the few students who went to my school, the only White person with whom I had direct interaction was the insurance man who stopped by our house each month to collect our premiums. Thinking back on this time, I struggled to come to understand how I was first *truly* introduced to the meaning of race and its prominence in the history of our nation.

As I continued to reflect, one particular instance came to mind—the encounter occurred while I was in the first grade when I became fully aware that I was Black. Initially, when the Martin Luther King Jr. Holiday was declared a national holiday, schools were not yet required to be closed, which was the case in my district. I recall my mother, and many other families in our neighborhood, making the conscious decision to keep us home from school that day to participate in the MLK march and celebration being held in our community. I recall asking my mother why I did not have to go to school, and she replied, "Today is Martin Luther King Day and you are not going to school because we have to go and participate in the march with our church. We *have* to go because without MLK you wouldn't have the opportunity to go to school anyway!" This experience was significant because until this time, my Blackness had not been emphasized in my home in a way that indicated that it was something about which I should be aware. That was not the first time my mother and I had conversed about Martin Luther King. There had been other talks. But this one was different. This time was more like the times educators refer to as "teachable moments." In this conversation, Martin Luther King's dynamism was placed in its appropriate context. I had already learned that he was a historical figure, but my mother deciding to keep me home from school as a display of reverence helped me to better understand his importance to our history.

This initial understanding of race was innocent, and I am fortunate that it was because, unfortunately, many others learned the functional meaning of race through much harsher circumstances. Sadly, countless individuals are not afforded with such a gentle initiation into racial consciousness. Instead, they are forced to make sense of unspeakable violence and cruelty on their way to developing a healthy sense of self. Steele (2010) noted that conditions of life tied to identity require individuals to reconcile their racial identities given, the ways in which such an identity can influence the outcome of a particular situation.

The conversation I had with my mom in the first grade led me to want to know more about my race. From that point on, I was more aware of the subtle reminders of my Blackness, but none significantly impacted my identity or my existence. Moments that had implications for my identity formation would come when I got older and began to venture outside of my nurturing home and neighborhood. For instance, my time in college at Bethune-Cookman University was filled with circumstances tied to identity, as race was a prominent component of my experience. Bethune-Cookman University is a historically Black university located in Daytona, Florida. Like most other historically Black colleges and universities (HBCUs), Bethune-Cookman's history was steeped in tradition. The rich tradition was evidence of the historical struggles in person of,

> small groups of the descendants of enslaved Africans, [who] through tenacity and hard work and in the face of openly racist policies and practices, made great sacrifices to achieve the academic and industrial advancements that gave them financial benefits, political influence, and social mobility—at least within the African American community and sometimes outside of it. (Gordon, 2012, p. 1)

The legacies of these brave souls did and still define HBCUs, and it is the custom of these institutions to share this legacy with students who attend.

I believe this was done in hopes of instilling in students a sense of respect for both Blackness and the institutions' history. In addition, communicating to students that the educational opportunities that were being provided should not be taken for granted was paramount. Whether it was through participating in structured discussions that took place during Wednesday morning at chapel services or by casual conversations between students and their faculty mentors and advisors, the (re)telling of the proud history of these institutions was always a resounding theme. As a result of my time at Bethune-Cookman, I gained a deeper appreciation of the Black experience and who I was as a Black male. More important, I learned the value of my culture and heritage. This was an important time for me because my earlier school experiences were void of this type of indoctrination. Also, this period in my life represented the origin of the heuristic I used to guide me through my continued attempts to negotiate my identity as a Black male. This is where I first picked up the sword and put on the shield.

PICKING UP THE SWORD, PUTTING ON THE SHIELD

Life at Bethune-Cookman was a significant time for me in terms of identity formation. It epitomizes the period when I began to reorient my thinking in terms of my racial identity and its impact on my life. This transition was not as subtle as when my mom explained the significance of MLK day to me in the first grade; this time it was intentionally more intrusive and explicit. In this space, we, as Black males, were collectively held to a higher standard. We were required to dress in a shirt and tie once a week for a professional seminar. In these seminars we vividly discussed standards of professional decorum, and a particular message was made very clear. The message was that because of our race, if we hoped to achieve the same results as our White counterparts, we had to prepare ourselves to work (at least) twice as hard. According to them, this cultural mandate would hold true regardless of the level of education we attain. This belief was impressed upon us with the reverence and solemnity of an old hymn. Consequently, it became so ingrained in me that I still carry it with me today. In these seminars I began to internalize the idea that the way I presented myself to others would have an impact on how they would perceive me, so presentation of self mattered in important ways.

When deconstructed, it is clear that the philosophy espoused by professors in these seminars evidenced their awareness of the stereotypes that can psychologically threaten Blacks (Aronson, Fried, & Good, 2002). According to Steele and Aronson (1995), this condition, known as the stereotype threat, entails being at risk of confirming as a self-characteristic, a negative stereotype about one's group. The knowledge of my professors of how Black males were perceived in society motivated them to reorient our thinking in ways that forced us to be aware of these stereotypes, too. Some of the negative stereotypes trafficked in the cultural meta-narrative construct deem Black males as lazy, less intelligent, aggressive, physically violent, deviant, and/or lacking self-control. Whether people believe or would be willing to admit this narrative, most individuals in our society are well aware of the many visceral stereotypes and images that surround us. The awareness of these negative stereotypes often elicits beliefs about and actions toward Black males.

Accompanying these stereotypes are certain stigmas that directly impact the formation of a healthy Black male identity. Banaji and Greenwald (2013) addressed this in their book *Blindspot: Hidden Biases of Good People*. In this text, they discussed how the stigmatization resulting from negative stereotypes impacts society and accompanies us at all times (Goffman, 2009). These authors contended that due to the stigmatization of Black males caused by harmful stereotypes, many have developed strategies to signal harmlessness. To me, Banaji and Greenwald's observations on stereotypes and the need for Black males to develop strategies to signal our harmlessness were auspicious, and after reflecting on their thoughts in relation to my personal experiences, I began to endorse this ideology as it had implications for my process of identity formation. Moreover, it provided me with a framework to ground my way of thinking about approaches to communicating my harmlessness.

In my continuing attempts to make meaning of this process of negotiation (figuring out my identity) and reconciliation (the accepting of things

I am forced to accept as being the way they are) of my identity as a Black male intellectual, I established the sword and the shield metaphor. This metaphor was dynamic for its distinctive capability for capturing my (un)conscious efforts to passively communicate my harmlessness while actively disabling stereotypes. The sword represents the offensive tactics I apply as a mechanism to actively confront the negative perceptions others may have developed about me due to their prolonged engagement with the meta-narrative. Conversely, the shield represents the defensive tactics utilized to deflect the potential responses of others resulting from this same engagement with the meta-narrative. The metaphor has also been refined over time, as I have become more conscious of the sociopsychological causes for its origins.

One of the earliest instances of consciously picking up the sword and putting on the shield was in my second year as a full-time doctoral student at a PWI. I was preparing to teach my first college course. During one of my regularly scheduled meetings with my faculty mentor, I discussed this new endeavor. During this time we had worked closely on several projects and had established a great relationship. The fact that such a relationship was forged was critical to this situation as it opened the door for authentic dialogue between us. In addition to providing me with several ideas about pedagogy, she encouraged me to be willing to present myself less business-like and stoic. Instead, she suggested that I attempt to be more personable when interacting with my prospective students. This piece of advice was at the same time interesting and perplexing as it caused me to wonder what led her to perceive me as being business-like. Was it the way I talked, acted, and dressed? I am guessing my facial expression communicated this to her because she then explained her thinking by explaining that upon initially meeting me, one may develop the impression that I am unapproachable. Obviously, if I were distant with my students such a demeanor would not be viewed as a relative strength of an instructor. However, based on her personal relationship with me, she knew that this interpretation of my actions was in direct contradiction to who I truly was as a person. As a mentee should with his mentor, I took her observations into consideration. The advice led to me making slight adjustments in the ways in which I interacted with my students, and I still heed to this advice today.

Nested within the conversation with my mentor were implications for the politics of power and identity. Essentially, I was being told that I needed to smile more in hopes of making people comfortable with me. Thus, their issues of discomfort were placed on my shoulders to manage. Unfortunately, this is a typical repercussion of the Black experience. Our identity is made problematic by others' (mis)perceptions, and, at the same time, our survival depends in some measure on our ability to meet them (more than) halfway to solve their issue.

RECONCILING IDENTITY AMID
STIGMATIZED SOCIAL STATUS

The vignette about Kingstan's school experience that I shared at the beginning of this narrative is particularly illustrative of how (mis)perception of
Black male behavior occurs and the associated potential costs of misperception. In his case, the costs could have been a loss of opportunity to participate
in a program for the gifted and talented. In other cases, these costs have been
much more severe such as the loss of life (see the Trayvon Martin, Michael
Brown, and Tamir Rice stories). Whether consciously or unconsciously, these
potential costs remain affixed to the minds of Black males as they engage in
their respective daily activities. In my case, the attentiveness to the potential
for cost begins when I rise in the morning to prepare myself to greet the world
that awaits me. Specifically, as a Black male, I consciously consider the ways
in which I (re)present myself to society. In my perspective, this is a necessary approach because of the negative interpretations associated with certain
articles of clothing (e.g., hoodies, sagging pants) when worn by Blacks. At
the same time, it is a frustrating double standard as White colleagues enjoy
the privilege of dressing as they wish without encumbering the same potential
costs or stigma. A failure to consider my attire could be costly. Therefore,
I have to be conscious of my clothing choices in relation to my day's events
and the places in which I will occupy.

Since my days at Bethune-Cookman, this level of consciousness of presentation is something I have carried with me. Throughout my professional
career, from my beginnings as a special education teacher to my current
position as an assistant professor, I have viewed the dynamics of costs and
(re)presentation with increasing levels of significance. At each phase of my
professional journey, I feel forced to consider the importance of how I present myself to others in the field—to both colleagues and students alike—as
being a fundamental ingredient in the recipe for professional success. I pay
particular attention to the ways I dress, speak, groom, and conduct myself.
Outside of my personal successes and the restrictions I have witnessed being
placed on others, I have little evidence to quantify this belief as being a reality. However, it is one that I have carried throughout even while sometimes
questioning its legitimacy.

An incident in which representation leapt to the forefront of my practice
occurred while teaching one of my courses. The focus for this particular
class session was culturally responsive teaching and how our beliefs about
diversity impact our work as teachers. As we discussed the significance of
how teachers' experience with race will have an impact on their practice, one
student shared that she had very little experience of working with individuals whose race was different from her own. In addition, the student shared
that she had never had a Black teacher before our class. At this time, another

student disclosed that she also had never had a Black teacher. The second student also added that upon learning that I was her professor for the course, she experienced significant levels of fear and anxiety. She then communicated that she had genuinely considered whether to remain in my section of the course or take another professor. Even though I understood that she had never had a Black instructor, I silently wondered why her first time having one would make her want to withdraw from the course. Was she just that uncomfortable with having a Black teacher or simply that uncomfortable with Black people? Apparently, this was not the case as the student explained that her feelings of apprehension about having me as an instructor were a result of the fact that she had recently been a victim of a violent crime at the hands of three Black males. Sadly, the student had been assaulted and robbed while walking from a store near the college campus. The student disclosed that since this horrifying event, she had been dealing with a fear of Black males. The student concluded her moment of sharing by stating that she was glad she remained in the course and her time with me had helped her to begin to resolve some of the issues and questions she previously had about Blacks.

Undergirding this interaction with my student is the issue of racial double standards. While acknowledging the reality that this student was unfortunately the victim of a violent crime, I also consider the following:

1. The student likely had numerous experiences with White males who were invalidating or, otherwise, hurtful, but she viewed these instances as isolated and not a representation of the group as a whole.
2. In each of those cases, the offending person was afforded the opportunity to be viewed as an individual who acted poorly. However, when it came to Black males, regardless of how extreme her situation was, she viewed it as somehow memetic of the character of all Black males.

The presence of a racial double standard in her situation is disturbing. Yet, when you consider the frequency with which this double standard of race occurs, it becomes even more problematic. Consequently, Black males are often placed in the untenable position to work to disprove the worst expectations while others are often judged based on their particular actions or decisions. There is no such thing as a neutral starting point for us. Instead, in most social interactions, we begin the race toward racial equity from a deficit position with strikes already levied against us. This lived cost of stigmatized Blackness is as true for me as a professor with a Ph.D. as it is for my son in the fourth grade hoping for a better educational opportunity. This cost results from the reality that the only characteristic of our identity that appears to matter most to others is our race. As a result, we are compelled to acknowledge that our Blackness—and all that is associated with it—remains the feature that is most symbolic of whom we are as individuals. This burdened contingency is what has materialized from society's continued exposure to the cultural meta-narrative informing them about us. The legitimacy of this reality enables us to better understand how Kingstan's teacher failed to recognize his unique abilities and why, in spite of my education and role in the academy, some individuals will continue to perceive me in such precarious ways.

This predicament is ignited by the ways in which we are often discussed in texts and in popular media. Baldwin (1984) spoke to this circumstance in his observations of the conditions he thought he faced as a Black writer in our society. He proclaimed:

> One of the difficulties about being a Negro writer . . . is that the Negro problem is written about so widely. The bookshelves groan under weight of information, and everyone therefore considers himself informed. And this information, furthermore, operates usually (generally, popularly) to reinforce traditional attitudes. (p. 6)

Baldwin's observations about the difficulty he faced as a writer still ring true today. In fact, I believe that this is true in every facet of society. My concerns of how the meta-narrative has impacted society's comprehension of Black males mirror Baldwin's apprehension about the manner in which Blacks have been written about in his time. These thoughts remain relevant today because of how the meta-narrative has been perpetuated and sustained (Harro, 2000). I contend that, in many cases, my success as a Black male academic and society at large hinges on my ability to negotiate the ascribed value for and responses to my Blackness. In short, my perceived professionalism (or lack thereof) will either provide evidence of the meta-narrative or serve as insight into its inadequacy.

DOUBLE-CONSCIOUSNESS AND THE ACADEMY

W. E. B. Du Bois first introduced "double-consciousness" in his attempts to describe the duality of self-consciousness of Blacks in America. In his discourse on the warring of the souls experienced by Blacks, Du Bois (1994) advanced the following:

> [The] Negro . . . in this American world,—a world which yields him no true self-consciousness, but only lets him see himself through the revelation of the other world. It is a peculiar sensation, this double-consciousness, this sense of always looking at one's self through the eyes of others, of measuring one's soul by the tape of a world that looks on in amused contempt and pity. One ever feels his two-ness,—an American, a Negro; two souls, two thoughts, two unreconciled

strivings; two warring ideals in one dark body, whose dogged strength alone keeps it from being torn asunder. (p. 2)

Upon learning of this philosophy of double-consciousness, I was better able to place my personal experiences in the broader context of Black male existence in our society. The construct of double-consciousness enabled me to reconcile many of the questions I had about some of the issues I had faced in life related to my racial identity.

Double-consciousness is an appropriate framework for describing the state of mind I possess as I navigate the predominantly White space in which I am currently situated as a faculty member. Others who have conducted research on faculty of color situated in these contexts have posited similar ideas. Stanley (2006) described this phenomenon as living in "two worlds" (p. 704), while Levin, Walker, Haberler, and Jackson-Boothby (2013) refer to it as the "the divided self" (p. 315). Such analogies are often used to describe the constant tension of being pulled between the faculty of color's ethnic or linguistic culture and the culture of the university. Each of these conceptualizations, remnants of Du Bois' characterization of double-consciousness, illustrates the predicament in which we, as faculty of color, find ourselves at PWIs. These conceptions of self aim to capture the feelings experienced by those of us who inhabit spaces that lack varying levels of cultural congruence.

Institutions of higher learning are greatly influenced by and cannot be separated from the larger social, historical, and cultural context in which they are nested (Allen, Epps, Guillory, Suh, & Bonous-Hammarth, 2000). Moreover, these institutions are a representation of the historically institutionalized struggles associated with or having a direct effect on how education has been shaped in our nation (Alvarez-McHatton, Glenn, Sue, & Gordon, 2012). As a Black male academic, I have come to understand that the manifestations of the meta-narrative about Black male potential has impacted society at large and can also be found in institutions of higher learning. While this issue has presented significant challenges for Black males throughout the American school system, it is often concentrated in the academy where the percentages of Black males existing are marginal as compared to other groups of individuals. I hold this belief because Black males continue to represent a small percentage of both the student and faculty population.

I contend that this matter has a significant social and psychological impact on those of us who remain in academe. The impact is pervasive and requires the individual to activate a mental resilience rarely required of others. While other members of the academy are able to fully immerse themselves in the process of becoming productive scholars, as a Black man, I must simultaneously attend to the demands of scholarly productivity as well as my unremitting pursuits to disqualify stereotypes.

As these authors professed, the degree to which Black males' (re)presentations of self conforms or departs from the broader "professional" standard is of paramount significance. As decisions regarding choices of hair, dress, and communication style prove to be mindless habits for some, over time, they have proven to be habits of mind for me. Even the ways in which we handle frustrations and disappointments in our roles as faculty are critical and must be well contemplated. I say this with my prior knowledge and understanding of the stereotypes of being violent and aggressive that accompany images of Black males (Sue et al., 2007). Hence, microscopic exhibitions of one's discomfort are interpreted as being hostile—even when an expression of discomfort or disagreement is warranted and commensurate with the offense.

I recall a situation that occurred in my department in which the leadership was implementing some changes to our workload. Lacking clarity on the proposed changes, I made several attempts to gain a better understanding by having conversations with multiple members of the leadership team. Unfortunately, my information-seeking attempts were perceived as being a challenge to the proposals. After gaining a sense that my actions were being misperceived, I halted my pursuit of understanding. In a subsequent conversation with one of my colleagues, who was also a woman of color, we discussed these issues as several others had the same questions and had also voiced their concerns. She shared with me that in recent weeks, she had noticed that I had become a bit reclusive and reserved. She based this on the fact that in several faculty meetings, I had refrained from giving my opinion on these issues as they were discussed corporately. Providing her with some situational context, I shared with her some anecdotes of my earlier meetings with members of the leadership team. After hearing my concerns, she recognized my position on the situation. Nonetheless, she encouraged me to try to avoid letting my disappointment show as it may be interpreted as me being an "angry Black man." While we laughed at her comments, we both recognized the uncomfortable truth in her remarks.

This situation is similar to the one I discussed about the student and the unfortunate crime that was committed on her by three Black males. In both instances, my behavior was going to represent either the stereotype or the counternarrative. Delgado (1989) affirmed that, counterstories possess significant power because they "can open new windows into reality, showing us that there are possibilities for life other than the ones we live" (p. 2414). In my case, as a faculty member in a PWI, I am not afforded with the opportunity to represent anything other than the counternarrative. While others can take such things as displays of emotion for granted, I must attend to their complexities. Even when on the surface, they appear so simplistic in nature.

Whether this issue is perceived or real, this represents a true concern for me and possibly other Black male faculty members. Regardless of the level of education we attain, we are still not viewed as simply a male with a Ph.D. Instead, we are viewed as a *Black male* with a Ph.D. More explicitly, a Black male with a Ph.D. who still has to contend with the stereotypes associated with my racial identity. Johnson (2001) discussed this *burdened truth* when noting that regardless of social status, we are still marked by the stigmatizable aspect of our social identity. Therefore, a White woman who is a lawyer is a "female lawyer"; this same lawyer, if Black, would be the "Black lawyer."

THE SWORD, THE SHIELD, AND THE TENURE PROCESS

In spite of the studies on the lived experiences of faculty of color as a whole in PWIs, little is known about how Black male faculty are experiencing the challenges of the tenure process. Absent from the discourse on the experiences of Black males in the academy are the voices that candidly discuss the tensions experienced during the preparation of the tenure portfolio. Some individuals have expressed concern about the "hidden or unwritten versus written rules" that govern this process (Stanley, 2006, p. 704). I share these concerns about this highly subjective, objective process. The *particulars* of the tenure process are rarely discussed corporately. However, sincere, more transparent conversations are often conducted in the quiet offices and halls of academia about the unpleasant nature of the tenure-earning process. The urban legends and horror stories can make an untenured faculty member feel even more vulnerable. If made public, these covert conversations would shed light on the tensions that countless faculty have due to their lack of knowledge regarding how tenure will be granted. Nonetheless, such exchanges rarely reach a communal level. Instead they percolate underneath the exterior, as questions remain unanswered.

As one can imagine, the subject of tenure causes a significant level of anxiety for the junior faculty member. When the dynamic of race is infused, this process can become even more psychologically exhausting. As I consider this issue, I am reminded of a scripture in the Bible. The scripture reads in part, "My people are destroyed for lack of knowledge" (Hosea 4:6, King James Version). Analogously, when there is a gap in the individual's knowledge base regarding the tenure process, he or she may be unsuccessful. In the same way the priests of the Biblical time failed to teach the Israelites God's word, some institutions have failed to adequately *teach* their tenure-seeking faculty the ingredients for success in the tenure process. We may not be destroyed, but failure to earn tenure may very well mean we perish from the academy.

Therefore, the silence surrounding the tenure process needs to be broken and greater transparency instituted in its stead. I provide this as a simple suggestion, but I recognize the potential costs of speaking on something that holds so much weight. Besides, who is going to be the first to speak? Who is willing to take that risk of openly acknowledging that they either do not understand or are fearful of the (hidden) tenure process? After all, we are each supposed to be intellectuals, experts, and scholars in our own right. In the highly competitive arena, that is academia, no one wants to present himself or herself as vulnerable. Acknowledgment and discussion of the emotions experienced while seeking tenure just may be what is needed to alleviate the junior faculty member's stress. At least I believe doing so would be helpful to me.

LOOKING BACK, LOOKING FORWARD

Over the years, the lived experiences of faculty of color in PWIs have garnered more attention. As a result, research in this area has grown and the voices of faculty of color are beginning to be heard. Some of the identified obstacles include the underrepresentation of faculty of color in U.S. colleges and universities, tendency to be overburdened with teaching and service responsibilities, inflexible expectations of universities about research and publications, and the low valuation of academic research related to racial/ ethnic dynamics (Allen et al., 2000). Depending on the particular context in which we are situated, each of these issues may affect us all differently. In addition, the level of mentorship and support a faculty member receives will be a mitigating factor in their efforts to overcome these obstacles.

In this chapter, I have attempted to detail some of the challenges that I have personally faced as a Black male in a PWI. In addition, I have discussed some of the approaches I have employed in my attempts to overcome them. Hopefully my narrative not only contributes to this literature but provides a new perspective to consider as it relates to the experiences of Black male academics. As I close my narrative detailing my existence as a Black male academic and my attempts to reconcile and negotiate my identity while simultaneously working toward tenure, I am left with several lingering questions. In a certain sense, the questions that remain are more penetrating now than before I began writing this chapter. I guess this is why Baldwin (1984) asserted:

> so before [we] can look forward in any meaningful sense, [we] must first be allowed to take a long look back. In the context of the Negro problem neither whites nor blacks, for excellent reasons of their own, have the faintest desire to look back; but I think the past is all that makes the present coherent, and further, that the past will remain horrible for exactly as long as we refuse to assess it honestly. (p. 6)

Taking that long look back that Baldwin discussed requires one to be coura-geous enough to confront the images and moments that might be revealed. At any rate, that intense reflection on the past must still occur. While looking back, I was able to make more sense of why I currently make many choices. However, some of the questions I now have relate to my son and his genera-tion. Specifically I wonder at what stage in his life will I begin to arm him with his sword and shield? As he watches me put on my literal shirt and tie, when will he understand that this literal shirt and tie also represents my figu-rative sword and shield? I want his initial awareness of his racial identity to be as gentle as it was for me and simultaneously fear that circumstances will force me to have a much more intense conversation. Ultimately, the goal in all of this is to minimize the potential costs of not being aware of his Black-ness. Whether I like it or not, the trajectory of racial progress seems to point to the inevitable moment when he will need to be fitted for his own sword and shield.

REFERENCES

Allen, W. R., Epps, E. G., Guillory, E. A., & Suh, S. A., & Bonous-Hammarth, M. (2000). The black academic: Faculty status among African Americans in U.S. higher education. *The Journal of Negro Education, 69*(1/2), 112–127.

Alvarez-McHatton, P., Glenn, T. L., Sue, & Gordon, K. (2012). The plight of special education leaders in challenging contexts: Purpose, potential, and possibility. *Journal of Special Education Leadership, 25*(1), 38–47.

Aronson, J., Fried, C. B., & Good, C. (2002). Reducing the effects of stereotype threat on African American college students by shaping theories of intelligence. *Journal of Experimental Social Psychology, 38*, 113–125.

Baldwin, J. (1984). *Notes of a native son.* Boston, MA: Beacon Press (original work published 1955).

Banaji, M. R., & Greenwald, A. G. (2013). *Blindspot: Hidden biases of good people.* New York, NY: Delacorte Press.

Delgado, R. (1989). Storytelling for oppositionist and others: A plea for narrative. *Michigan Law Review, 87*(8), 2411–2441.

Du Bois, W. E. B. (1994). *The souls of black folk.* New York, NY: Dover Publications (original work published 1903).

Goffman, E. (2009). *Stigma: Notes on the management of spoiled identity.* New York, NY: Simon and Schuster.

Gordon, B. M. (2012). "Give a brotha a break!": The experiences and dilemmas of middle-class African American male students in white suburban schools. *Teachers College Record, 114*, 1–26.

Harro, B. (2000). The cycle of socialization. In M. Adams, W. J. Blumenfeld, R. Cas-taneda, H. W. Hackman, M. L. Peters, & X. Zuniga (Eds.), *Readings for diversity and social justice* (pp. 15–21). New York, NY: Routledge.

Johnson, A. G. (2001). *Privilege, power, and difference.* Boston, MA: McGraw-Hill.

Levin, J. S., Walker, L., Haberler, Z., & Jackson-Boothby, A. (2013). The divided self: The double consciousness of faculty of color in community colleges. *Community College Review, 41*(4), 311–329.

Stanley, C. A. (2006). Coloring the academic landscape: Faculty of color breaking the silence in predominantly White colleges and universities. *American Educational Research Journal, 43*(4), 701–736.

Steele, C. M. (2010). *Whistling vivaldi: How stereotypes affect us and what we can do.* New York, NY: W.W. Norton.

Steele, C. M., & Aronson, J. (1995). Stereotype threat and the intellectual test performance of African Americans. *Journal of Personality and Social Psychology, 69*(5), 797–811.

Sue, D. W., Capodilupo, C. M., Torino, G. C., Bucceri, J. M., Holder, A., Nadal, K. L., & Esquilin, M. (2007). Racial microaggressions in everyday life: Implications for clinical practice. *American Psychologist, 62*(4), 271.

Tatum, B. D. (1997). *"Why are all the Black kids sitting together in the cafeteria?": And other conversations about race.* New York, NY: Basic Books.

Thomson, R. G. (1997). *Extraordinary bodies: Figuring physical disability in American culture and literature.* New York, NY: Columbia University Press.

Chapter 4

Navigating Higher Education as an Asian Immigrant Female

Sohyun An

I am an Asian immigrant woman teaching at a predominantly White institution of higher education in the southern United States. At the beginning of this writing, I had just turned in my tenure and promotion portfolio for review. Although daunting, preparing the portfolio and making a case for my work provided me time to reflect on my journey, which is a tale of how a model student/citizen of South Korea evolved into a teacher educator of social justice education in the United States. As I was tracing my trajectory, I felt empowered and obligated to share my story with others who are in a similar situation to mine and may find my story relevant.

Thus, this is a narrative of how transnational learning and living has shaped my consciousness as a teacher educator who is committed to social justice education and how I interrogate the challenges and possibilities I encounter as an Asian immigrant woman who, through her role as an educator, advocates for antiracism, antioppression, and social action in a primarily White U.S. higher education system. In the following text, I recount my journey from my childhood and upbringing in South Korea to my young adulthood as an international graduate student in the United States to my current situation as an assistant professor working toward tenure and promotion in the Deep South.

The story is embedded in my theoretical engagement with critical race theory (Bell, 1995; Delgado, 1995; Delgado & Stefancic, 2001; Matsuda, 1995), Asian American studies (Chang, 1993; Espiritu, 2008; Lee, 1996; Lowe, 1996; Museus, 2013; Takaki, 1998; Tuan, 1998; Wu, 2002), critical multicultural education (Kincheloe & Steinberg, 1997; McLaren, 1997; Sleeter & Grant, 2003), and global citizenship education (Bigelow & Peterson 2000; Gaudelli, 2009; Kasai & Merryfield, 2004; Myers, 2006; Nussbaum, 1996). Agreeing with the power of interpretive autobiography and reflective inquiry to investigate lived experiences (Angrosino, 1989; Denzin, 1997; van Manen,

1990), I use my personal experience and autobiographic voice (Creswell, 1998; Davis, 1999) to narrate the story. The account is based on my own recollections of and reflections on my transnational lived experience and a close reading of documents, such as my journals, student course evaluations, meeting minutes, and e-mail communications.

GROWING UP IN SOUTH KOREA

I grew up in South Korea during the 1980s. A typical day, during my primary school years, began by pledging allegiance to the flag of South Korea and singing the national anthem. In front of the classroom, the photo of then president Chun Doo-Hwan hung next to Taegeukgi (the South Korean flag) on the wall. Based on his photograph, I thought our president appeared to be a nice and kind man. It was not until in college that I learned about the dictatorship and gross injustice of his regime and the other authoritarian presidents of my home country. I grew up watching U.S. president Ronald Reagan on TV news and thinking he was a handsome and great world leader who was diligently protecting us from communist North Korea. It was not until I came to the United States as an adult that I saw a more realistic view of the United States and its role in world politics. I grew up watching the Olympics and the World Cups, shedding happy tears with my parents and siblings when our team or athletes beat Japan or China. I remember being very proud when I won an award in my school's anti-Communism poster competition. I drew U.S. soldiers fighting for us, South Korea, against communist North Korea and the Chinese army. I wrote, "Let's not forget about 6.25 [the Korean War]. Our hero is America; our enemy is communist North Korea!"

As such, my childhood and early education in the 1980s were largely shaped by the dominant ideologies of that historic era in South Korea, including anticommunist nationalism, pro-Americanism, and anti-Japanese and anti-Chinese sentiments (Kim, 2006). During the 1990s, my country was going through profound political and economic changes in the midst of the end of the Cold War; the death of Kim Il-sung (the first president of North Korea); electing the first civilian president after 32 years of military rule; and the 1997 financial crisis (Kim, 2010). However, the dominant discourses continued, and my college education was not transformative; therefore, it did not challenge the oppressive norms of mainstream South Korean society. Throughout my education in South Korea, I was a model student who respected her teachers, followed the school rules, studied hard, and received good grades. I was also a model citizen who never questioned the authority or the dominant social values. In retrospect, my upbringing has significantly influenced my experiences in the United States and how I became the person I am today, which I will talk about next.

ENTERING THE UNITED STATES

I came to the United States to pursue my doctoral degree in the early 2000s. The desire to be educated in the United States has long been prevalent in South Korean society because of the power and privilege of the U.S. knowledge regime. The national formation of South Korea and its development into the current state has been deeply impacted by the United States. The U.S. Army's military occupation of Korea after World War II and the country's involvement in the Korean War played enormous roles in shaping almost every domain of South Korean society, thereby solidifying the political, economic, cultural, and educational influence of the United States over South Korea (Rhee, 2006). The privilege of highly ranked U.S. university degrees has provided better job opportunities, social respect, and economic returns for citizens in South Korean society (Abelmann, Park, & Kim, 2009). Enticed by the allegedly superior and professional status of U.S. academia, I joined the incessant and increasing flow of South Korean students to U.S. graduate schools in the early 2000s. Like many, I planned to get a doctoral degree from a prestigious U.S. university and come back home and live a successful life in my country.

My original plan changed, however. Seven years of living and studying in the United States transformed my thoughts about the United States, South Korea, the world, and myself. I got to see other faces of the United States, which was far from the illusion I learned and imagined—the world's richest, most democratic, freest, and most advanced country spreading and protecting democracy, freedom, and peace throughout the world. It was shocking to see how many children in this rich country were homeless. It was surprising to see that "racism is normal, not aberrant in American society" (Delgado, 1995, p. xiv). It was confusing to learn that Whites and Blacks are not the only Americans; Hispanics/Latin@s and Asians are also legitimate citizens of the United States. More perplexing yet was to see how Latinos and Asians are discriminated against as "undocumented," "illegal," and "foreigners" when, for many of them, this is the only home they have ever known. It was confusing to see how dissents against the government's reaction to September 11 were oppressed when I had thought that America is the land of freedom, including the right to free speech, and the protector of world peace and democracy. As I experienced the real United States in real time, I became disoriented at first and disillusioned in the end.

I also became confused and disenchanted as I faced the racism, blind patriotism, and oppression of my ideologies and those of my home country through transnational living and studying in the United States. Growing up in South Korea, where being Korean meant being against Japan and China, I had never identified myself with Japanese or Chinese, and I was frustrated when Americans didn't distinguish me from immigrants of Chinese and

Japanese origins and lumped me together with them as "Asian." I slowly realized how oppressive this thinking was. I felt duped by my own country and its civic education, which was far from liberating or promoting humanity, but instead nationalist, as well as oppressive and racist toward others. As I crossed physical and psychological borders between the United States and South Korea, I became more and more conscious of the oppressive, undemocratic, and inhumane nature of the oppressive nationalism and racism that was entrenched in both the educational system and the larger society of my country.

These disorienting and often-frustrating experiences directed me into literature on race, history, citizenship, and education. I delved into critical race theory (Bell, 1995; Delgado, 1995; Delgado & Stefancic, 2001; Matsuda, 1995), Asian American studies (Chang, 1993; Espiritu, 2008; Lee, 1996; Lowe, 1996; Museus, 2013; Takaki, 1988; Tuan, 1998; Wu, 2002), critical multicultural education (Kincheloe & Steinberg, 1997; McLaren, 1997; Sleeter & Grant, 2003), and global citizenship education (Bigelow & Peterson, 2000; Gaudelli, 2009; Kasai & Merryfield, 2004; Myers, 2006; Nussbaum, 1996) to make sense of where, how, and why racism, nationalism, and other ideologies of mine, my country, and the United States come from and what I can do to contribute to undoing the legacy of oppression and injustice. After all, my experiential learning in the transnational space between South Korea and the United States transformed my consciousness of power, privilege, race, citizenship, and education.

It is this newly emerged consciousness that changed how I perceive myself, as well as my personal and professional identity as a teacher educator for social justice education. I felt empowered and obligated to participate in and provide an education that is far from what I had. My newly established goal as a teacher educator was to empower future teachers and their young students as antiracist and justice-oriented citizens at both the local and global level.

NAVIGATING U.S. HIGHER EDUCATION

Success and Challenges in My Own Classroom

I entered my current location, a primarily White university in the U.S. South, six years ago. My major teaching responsibility has been to teach three sections of an elementary social studies methods course each semester. Building on scholarship on teaching social studies for social justice (Agarwal-Rangnath, 2013; Au, 2009; Banks, 1999; DeLeon & Ross, 2010; Epstein, 2009; Stanley, 2005; Tyson & Park, 2006; Wade, 2007), my goal in teaching elementary social studies methods has focused on assisting my students, who will soon be elementary school teachers, in developing conceptual and pedagogical tools to teach social studies for social justice.

Not surprisingly but nevertheless unfortunately, the official knowledge embodied in school curricula transmits the values, knowledge, and ideologies of the dominant group and supports the status quo (Anyon, 1979; Apple, 1992). In U.S. history/social studies textbooks, almost everyone is White, male, middle class, Christian, and heterosexual; the United States is a land of wealth and opportunity in which anyone can get what he or she works for; racism and other oppressions existed in the past, but they have been solved by the generous good deeds of presidents; and the United States is a world leader in spreading democracy and freedom and fighting against totalitarian, communist, or terrorist countries (Anyon, 1979; Chappell, 2010; Cruz, 2002; Fitzgerald, 1980; Ladson-Billings, 2003; Loewen, 1995; Romanowski, 2009; Schmidt, 2012; Sleeter & Grant, 1991).

In light of the foregoing, my goal has been to challenge my students to examine whose voices, experiences, and knowledge are left out of such a dominant narrative, uncover the hegemonic status-quo norms of sociohistorical knowledge, and explore their own roles in relation to social problems (Agarwal-Rangnath, 2013; Au, 2009; Hursh & Ross, 2000). I have sought to engage my students and, ultimately, their future students in a critical analysis of their societies and the social action they have taken to counteract oppression and promote social justice (Wade, 2007). I have also attempted to help my students reconstruct the definition of good citizenship by moving away from passive, obedient, and uncritically patriotic citizenship to active, questioning, and critically patriotic citizenship (Westheimer, 2009; Westheimer & Kahne, 2004).

I am truly thankful that, through my doctoral program, I evolved into a teacher educator who is committed to social studies education for social justice. However, I wasn't prepared for the pedagogy to engage my students in the difficult work of deconstructing and reconstructing official knowledge. I graduated with no experience in teaching a college class. Although I heard about students' resistance to courses that challenge their belief systems, I innocently thought my hard work and caring would save me from harsh student resistance. I was naively optimistic. During my first semester of teaching, I was accused of being radical, anti-American, communist, or crazy. It was a real learning experience.

Most of my students were White, Christian, and female. Many were from military families with strong pride in being American. Most of them had never been outside the United States and planned to return to their rural or suburban communities to teach. Unsurprisingly, most of them had never had an immigrant Asian female as their teacher or professor before. Now, they were facing a professor who is from "elsewhere" in Asia, an atheist, a nonnative English speaker, and frequent border-crossing migrant. To my students, I was absolutely "the other" with whom they had almost nothing in common. Schmidt (2002) stated, "The common associations of language with race and national origin create an ideological context in the U.S. where Americans speaking languages other than English, and whose origins lie in continents other than Europe, are racialized as alien outsiders, as *Others*" (p. 142, emphasis in the original). The image of others is frequently equated with inferiority.

Like many other Asian female faculty in the literature (Amos, 2014; Han, 2014; Liang, 2006; Shrake, 2006), my accented English made my students suspicious about my credibility as their professor. Several students gave me a low score in their course evaluation, commenting, "Although Dr. An means well, she needs to improve her English" and "It was very hard to understand the professor." One student said at the end of the semester,

> To be honest, I wanted to switch to another section when I first saw your name listed as the instructor. But I couldn't because only this section fit my schedule. But, it turned out great. Although sometimes it was hard to understand, I know you worked very hard and the course was really thought provoking.

This student was one of only a few who viewed my course, overall, in a positive light.

Along with my students' criticism of my "broken English," another popular source of their discontent derived from the nature of the course. I explained on the first day, "In this course, we will delve into race, religion, wars, LGBT issues, capitalism, colonialism, and sexism as important topics/concepts in social studies and learn pedagogical ways to engage elementary students in critical analyses of them." Many students seemed to think, "She must be crazy. These issues are too controversial, too complex! It's too inappropriate for young, innocent children!" Students wrote in the course evaluation: "This is a social studies methods course! It's not a diversity course! We took that course already!" "She didn't teach us how to make social studies fun! What we mostly did was talk and discuss social issues!" "Dr. An did a great job at raising our awareness of various issues. But I don't agree with her communist ideas. This is America. If she hates capitalism, she should go back to China!"

These comments were extremely painful. I rehearsed each lesson several times in front of a mirror so that my language would not become a barrier that kept me from reaching my students. I explicitly explained several times that we first needed to deconstruct and reconstruct meaningful social studies curricula before moving on to "fun" activities. However, my students taught me, during that first semester, that this was not enough. I had to find different ways to engage my students. I asked my colleagues and reviewed literature in a search for what teacher educators like me, "the others" in a primarily White college classroom, do to address these issues and how.

Building on experiences and insights from those who trekked this less-traveled road prior to me (Amos, 2014; Han, 2014; Kubota, 2002; Rong, 2002; Zong, 2006), I first changed my readings. Rather than dry, scholarly articles, I began to use teachers' vignettes so that my students could relate to the reading and see that teachers like themselves can teach "tough," "too controversial" concepts and ideas in social studies. To address my questioned authority and credibility as an Asian female with a nonnative English accent, I decreased my talking time by using video clips, songs, films, and other visual/audio material, speaking instead through White, native English speakers' voices. To create equal democratic relations, I began to give my students more space and time to choose what they wanted to dig deeper into and peer teach. I began to meet with my students individually or as a small group before and after class to build rapport with them. I also began to be transparent, even vulnerable, with my students to make our classroom a safe place to share what we think, feel, wonder, and struggle with. I talked about my own racism, homophobia, ethnocentrism, nationalism, and colonialism, which I used to have, as well as how I began to unlearn, where I am now, and what I am doing to constantly become a less oppressive and more justice-oriented educator and citizen.

When I think more about it, these strategies are just good pedagogy, and there is nothing new or unique in them. But for me, an Asian female with whom her students rarely find anything in common, these pedagogies have become a prerequisite to having a constructive learning experience for both my students and me.

Although it became less and less challenging to engage my students in discussions of "tough," "controversial," and "uncomfortable" topics in elementary social studies, there is one area that continues to be challenging: rethinking patriotism and U.S. military action throughout the world. When it comes to talking about what, how, and why to teach about wars in which the United States has engaged in the past and the present, my students, although not all, fall silent. For instance, when the course is on why, what, and how to teach about September 11, I become an absolute other to my students, an outsider who is accusing their proud, beloved country of doing injustice to other parts of the world. To them, I am anti-American. Most of my students were in upper elementary or middle school when that tragic event happened. As witnesses who lived this event in history, my students have vivid memories and associated emotions about the event. While sharing their lived experiences and their plans to teach about this moment in history, many focus on the fact that their innocent, beloved country was attacked and develop lesson plans that focus on the importance of unity and patriotism. To them, my invitation to dig deeper into the event, including an examination of the historical sociopolitical origins of the event and the various consequences of the event upon different groups in and beyond the nation, sounds suspicious. I feel the questioning eyes of my students, who seem to think, "She is anti-American!"

I am still searching for a pedagogy that works for me and my students on this issue. hooks (1994) reminded me that "in the transformed classroom, there is often a much greater need to explain philosophy, strategy, intent than in the 'norm' setting" (p. 42). Indeed, engaging in progressive pedagogies is not easy and not without discomfort and uncertainty. Whenever I am anxious and frustrated with my students' resistance, I remind myself of my own experience. Yes, it took real physical and psychological border crossing and many years of unlearning and learning for me to become reflective upon me, my country, and the world. I keep in mind that it takes time for one to rethink, reexamine, and critically evaluate the beliefs and worldviews that one has long grown up with and been exposed to.

Struggles beyond Classroom

To my surprise, service turned out to be the most challenging aspect of my work. As I continue to teach, I have been making progress and developing my own "engaged pedagogy" (hooks, 1994), which "respects and cares for the souls of students . . . to provide the necessary conditions where learning can most deeply and intimately occur" (p. 13). Regarding research, despite the challenge of finding time to conduct research and write in English, which is not my mother language, research is at least a battle with myself. In contrast, service is, I found, a battle in which I must fight against my institution and its institutional racism.

To achieve tenure and promotions in my current institution, I need to prove the significance and quality of my service and emerging leadership. So, after my first year of teaching, which was a dramatic learning curve, I began to look for opportunities to serve and lead. Before too long, I discovered that my position as an Asian female immigrant teaching social studies is of little value in my institution.

For instance, I realized I was rarely being selected or invited for service. In contrast, I was often hearing other junior faculty, or even those hired after me, express discontent with "too much service." One day, a White junior faculty member shared her frustration with being asked to serve too much: "I have no time for my research. I am on six committees and I am chairing two of them. Almost every day, I have a meeting. It's just too much service." Truly, I thought her concerns and complaints legitimate. As junior faculty, we should be protected from too much service expectations so that we can focus on teaching and research before taking on leadership roles. On the other hand, I was distressed. To me, the unequal opportunity seemed related to institutional beliefs about me and my ability or qualification to serve. One year after another, the message sent to me has become clear: being an Asian female who teaches elementary social studies has little to offer to my current institution.

First, I am not White. I am not Black. I am an Asian in the Deep South. Like many other places in the United States, discussions about race in my institution are constructed on a White–Black dichotomy (Lee, 2005; Wu, 2002), in which "'American' means 'white' and 'minority' means 'black'" (Wu, 2002, p. 20). Asian Americans are "perpetual foreigners" (Wu, 2002, p. 81) or "forever foreigners" (Tuan, 1998, p. 18) who are not authentic Americans. In this line of thought, the issues of diversity almost automatically translate into race issues, which automatically mean African American issues. Indeed, there is no room for Asians in the discussion of diversity or race.

For instance, last year, my institution invited two scholars as an initiative to address diversity issues. Both scholars were African Americans, and their presentations and follow-up discussions centered on issues of race from an African American perspective. By saying this, I don't mean that African American issues are not important. On the contrary, it is a very urgent and critical issue; teacher educators, researchers, and concerned citizens should engage in fighting against institutional and individual racism against African Americans. What I am trying to say is that there is almost zero institutional awareness and interest in racism against Asians in the United States and its complicated relation to other forms of racism and oppression in general. As another example, my institution has a strategic goal to recruit teacher candidates of color, and one of its initiatives is inviting K–12 students from "diverse" schools to the campus. Faculty members of color are asked to participate in the event as role models to students of color, thereby inspiring them to do well in school and think of being educators as a career. I was unaware of this annual event until an African American colleague expressed her struggle with being asked to participate in the event every year. I could see how hard it would be for a junior faculty member to say no to an institutional request to serve the institution for such a good cause. On the other hand, I was disheartened by my institution's limited definition of students of color and faculty of color.

At the core of these two cases is the idea that Asians have nothing to do with diversity or race issues. Despite the more than 150-year history of Asians in the United States, and although the United States is the country of immigrants, Asians are not incorporated into the collective memory of who qualifies as an American or American minority (Lee, 2005; Takaki, 1988; Tuan, 1998; Wu, 2002). In this thinking, why do we have to care about Asians when they are not real Americans? In addition to this nativist racism that excludes Asians from the definition of American, the model minority myth that lumps Asian Americans together as a successful, hardworking, and compliant minority also contributes to the invisibility of Asians in discourses on diversity and race issues (Chang, 1993; Lee, 1996; Wu, 2002). According to this line of thought, why should we care about Asians when they do well in school? The fact that many Asian students are poor, many are struggling in school, and many are bullied and discriminated against is not seen, heard, or publicized (Ng, Lee, & Park, 2007). It masks extreme inequalities within and between different Asian groups in the United States and diverts public attention from the existence of discrimination (Chang, 1993; Wu, 2002). In short, the nativist racism against Asians, such as Asian as forever foreigners or a model minority, is embedded in my institution's work on diversity and antiracism in education. As a result, this leads to little opportunity for me to serve.

Second, I am not teaching literacy, math, or STEM (Science, Technology, Engineering, and Mathematics) subjects. I am teaching social studies. The marginalized status of social studies in the elementary school curriculum translates into the marginalized status of social studies in teacher education (Bolick, Adams, & Willox, 2010; Fry, 2009). In the post-NCLB (No Child Left Behind) era, which relies on high-stakes testing in reading and mathematics as the primary measurement of student and school improvement (Au, 2009; McGuire, 2007), in today's nationwide push for STEM education (Obama, 2015), social studies in elementary education is almost a disappearing subject (Boyle-Baise, Hsu, Johnson, Serriere, & Stewart, 2008; Center on Education Policy, 2008; Fitchett & Heafner, 2010). This, then, leads to little investment in teacher education for elementary social studies (Passe, 2006). The arrival of edTPA (American Association of Colleges of Teacher Education, 2014), the high-stakes, standardized preservice teacher assessment, has furthered the marginalization of social studies in my elementary teacher education program. The elementary edTPA tests teacher candidates' content pedagogy in literacy and math but not in social studies. After edTPA became the requirement for teaching certification in the state where I teach, I have been seeing our institutional resources move more and more toward preparation for edTPA and less and less on elementary social studies in our teacher education program. This means there is little opportunity for me to serve my institution because my expertise in social studies is not an "urgent" need.

In short, my position as an Asian faculty member who teaches elementary social studies methods is valued very little in my institution, leaving me with little opportunity to serve and prove the significance of my service and leadership. I see very clearly that, if I do not actively seek out service opportunities, I will be evaluated very poorly in the service area. Previous studies have shown that culturally and linguistically diverse faculty are rarely selected as leaders and, thus, are not on decision-making teams (Han, 2012; Stanley,

2006); in particular, female Asian faculty generally occupy the junior ranks and have one of the lowest tenure rates in academia (Hune, 1998).

To survive, I must sign up whenever there is a call for service. Equally important is that I sign up so that my service will hopefully challenge, instead of reproduce, stereotypes of Asians such as Asians are passive, are forever foreign, and lack leadership. I do not want to unwittingly participate in subordination by taking on the dominant society's nativist racism and oppressive model minority myth regarding Asian Americans. Through my active service and working with other colleagues, I attempt to break the stereotypes. I view my efforts as acts of intervention to rupture the forces of marginalization and silencing. Thus, I am currently engaged in battle with the nativist racism that is embedded in my current institution.

WHAT KEEPS ME GOING?

Recently, I received the official letter stating that I have been given tenure and promotion. I was very excited, but at the same time I felt very exhausted. For the past six years, I have constantly been running to prove the quality and significance of my work in teaching and serving on the weekdays and in researching every weekend. I was an absent mother of two young children who have not been happy with their mom "always working and working" with "no time to play with us [my children]!" Although going through a tenure and promotion process is never easy for anybody (Loo & Ho, 2006; Samimy, 2006), I felt my battle was extremely tiring due to my position in my current location and that my juggling was even more intense because I am an immigrant Asian faculty member who had to do more than her non-Asian, non-foreign colleagues because of her questioned credibility, qualification, legitimacy, and quality.

Albeit exhausting, the past six years were another transformative learning experience for me. My students, colleagues, institution, and the way they treated and interacted with me have taught me both the limitations and potential of my work toward teacher education for social justice–oriented social studies. Although often frustrated and defeated by seemingly invincible nativist racism from my students and my institution, I saw the changes I have made through my teaching and service. Comments such as "Dr. An, this course has been very thought-provoking and changed the way I think about social studies . . . You helped me rethink my beliefs and the social norms. . . . I'd like to bring multiple perspectives to my future students!" or "Dr. An, your presentation on college pedagogy was very well received by faculty who attended the workshop. We look forward to working with you in the near future!" keep me going.

Whenever I am disappointed by the limitations of the changes that I have
made, I remind myself that transformative learning won't happen overnight,
after one course, or through one project. For me, it took almost seven years
and various painful moments to finally transform myself and my racist,
oppressive thinking. It took several physical and psychological border cross-
ings between the United States and South Korea, combined with dialogic and
nurturing spaces of unlearning and new learning.

So I am tired, I am exhausted, I struggle, but I carry on! My transnational
education, physical and psychological border crossing, and critical engagement with critical race theory, AsianCrit, and social justice–oriented social
studies education have shaped my consciousness as a teacher educator who
is committed to antiracist, justice-oriented citizenship education and have
enabled me to translate theoretical concepts into everyday practice in teaching and serving. I hope this analysis of my own experiences will shed light
on questions of a much wider scope regarding how to educate future teachers and, ultimately, their young students to become justice-oriented citizens.

REFERENCES

Abelmann, N., Park, S. J., & Kim, H. (2009). College rank and neoliberal subjectivity
in South Korea: The burden of self-development. *Inter-Asia Cultural Studies, 10*(2),
229–247.

Agarwal-Rangnath, R. (2013). *Social studies, literacy, and social justice in the common core classroom.* New York, NY: Teachers' College Press.

American Association of Colleges of Teacher Education. (2014). *edTPA overview.*
Retrieved from http://edtpa.aacte.org/about-edtpa

Amos, Y. T. (2014). To lose is to win: The effects of student evaluations in a multicultural education class on a Japanese faculty with a non-native English accent.
Understanding & Dismantling Privilege, 4(2), 117–133.

Angrosino, M. V. (1989). *Documents of interaction: Biography, autobiography, and
life history in social science perspective.* Gainesville: University of Florida Press.

Anyon, J. (1979). Ideology and United States history textbooks. *Harvard Educational
Review, 49*(3), 361–386.

Apple, M. (1992). Do the standards go far enough? Power, policy, and practice in
mathematics education. *Journal for Research in Mathematics Education, 23*(5),
412–431.

Au, W. (2009). High-stakes testing and discursive control: The triple bind for nonstan-
dard student identities. *Multicultural Perspectives, 11*(2), 65–71.

Banks, J. A. (1999). *An introduction to multicultural education* (2nd ed.). Boston, MA:
Allyn and Bacon.

Bell, D. (1995). Who's afraid of critical race theory? *University of Illinois Law
Review, 4,* 893–910.

Bigelow, B., & Peterson, B. (2000). *Rethinking globalization: Teaching for justice in
an unjust world.* Milwaukee, WI: Rethinking Schools Press.

Bolick, C. M., Adams, R. L., & Willox, L. (2010). The marginalization of elementary social studies in teacher education. *Social Studies Research & Practice, 5*(1), 1–22.

Boyle-Baise, L., Hsu, M., Johnson, S., Serriere, S. C., & Stewart, D. (2008). Putting reading first: Teaching social studies in the elementary classroom. *Theory and Research in Social Education, 36*(3), 233–255.

Center on Education Policy. (2008). *How state and federal accountability policies have influenced curriculum and instruction in three states.* Washington, DC: Author.

Chang, R. S. (1993). Toward an Asian American legal scholarship: Critical race theory, poststructuralism, and narrative space. *California Law Review, 19,* 1243–1323.

Chappell, D. (2010). Training Americans: Ideology, performance, and social studies textbooks. *Theory and Research in Social Education, 38*(2), 248–269.

Creswell, J. W. (1998). *Qualitative inquiry and research design: Choosing among five traditions.* Thousand Oaks, CA: Sage.

Cruz, B. C. (2002). Don Juan and rebels under palm trees: Depictions of Latin Americans in US history textbooks. *Critique of Anthropology, 22*(3), 323–342.

Davis, C. A. (1999). *Reflective ethnography.* London, UK: Association of Social Anthropologists.

DeLeon, A., & Ross, E. W. (Eds.). (2010). *Critical theories, radical pedagogies, and social education: Towards new perspectives for the social studies.* Rotterdam, The Netherlands: Sense Publishers.

Delgado, R. (Ed.). (1995). *Critical race theory: The cutting edge.* Philadelphia, PA: Temple University Press.

Delgado, R., & Stefancic, J. (2001). *Critical race theory: An introduction.* New York, NY: New York University Press.

Denzin, N. K. (1997). *Interpretive ethnography.* Thousand Oaks, CA: Sage.

Epstein, T. (2009). *Interpreting national history: Race, identity and pedagogy in classrooms and communities.* New York, NY: Routledge Press.

Espiritu, Y. L. (2008). *Asian American women and men: Labor, laws, and love.* Lanham, MD: Rowman & Littlefield.

Fitchett, P. G., & Heafner, T. L. (2010). A national perspective on the effects of high-stakes testing and standardization on elementary social studies marginalization. *Theory and Research in Social Education, 38,* 114–130.

Fitzgerald, F. (1980). *America revised: History schoolbooks in the twentieth century.* Boston, MA: Little, Brown and Co.

Fry, S. (2009). On borrowed time: How four elementary preservice teachers learned to teach social studies in the NCLB era. *Social Studies Research and Practice, 4*(1), 31–41.

Gaudelli, W. (2009). Heuristics of global citizenship discourses towards curriculum enhancement. *Journal of Curriculum Theorizing, 25*(1), 68–85.

Han, K. T. (2012). Experiences of faculty of color teaching in a predominantly White university: Fostering interracial relationships among faculty of color and White preservice teachers. *International Journal of Progressive Education, 8*(2), 25–48.

Han, K. T. (2014). Moving racial discussion forward: A counterstory of racialized dynamics between an Asian-woman faculty and White preservice teachers in traditional rural America. *Journal of Diversity in Higher Education, 7*(2), 126–146.

hooks, b. (1994). *Teaching to transgress.* New York, NY: Routledge.

Hune, S. (1998). *Asian Pacific American women in higher education: Claiming visibility and voice.* Washington, DC: Association of American Colleges and Universities.

Hursh, D., & Ross, E. W. (2000). *Democratic social studies: Social studies for social change.* New York, NY: Falmer Press.

Kasai, M., & Merryfield, M. M. (2004). How are teachers responding to globalisation. *Social Education, 68,* 354–359.

Kim, E. (2006). Korean political culture and U.S.–Korean relations. *US–Korea Institute Yearbook* (pp. 59–69). Washington, DC: Johns Hopkins University.

Kim, H. (2010). A brief history of the U.S.-ROK alliance and anti-Americanism in South Korea. *Shorenstein APARC Research, 31*(1), 25–37.

Kincheloe, J., & Steinberg, S. (1997). *Changing multiculturalism.* Philadelphia, PA: Open University Press.

Kubota, R. (2002). Marginality as an asset: Toward a counter-hegemonic pedagogy for diversity. In L. Vargas (Ed.), *Women faculty of color in the white classroom: Narratives on the pedagogical implications of teacher diversity* (pp. 293–307). New York, NY: Peter Lang.

Ladson-Billings, G. (2003). Lies my teacher still tells: Developing a critical perspective toward social studies. In G. Ladson-Billings (Ed.), *Critical race theory perspectives on social studies* (pp. 1–11). Greenwich, CT: Information Age.

Lee, S. J. (1996). *Unraveling the model minority stereotype.* New York, NY: Teachers College Press.

Lee, S. J. (2005). *Up against whiteness.* New York, NY: Teachers College Columbia University.

Liang, X. (2006). Professing in a nonnative tongue. In G. Li & G. Beckett (Eds.), *Strangers of the academy: Asian women scholars in higher education* (pp. 85–104). Sterling, VA: Stylus Publishing.

Loewen, J. (1995). *Lies my teacher told me.* New York, NY: Touchstone/Simon and Schuster.

Loo, C., & Ho, H. (2006). Asian American in the academy. In G. Li & G. Beckett (Eds.), *Strangers of the academy: Asian women scholars in higher education* (pp.134–162). Sterling, VA: Stylus Publishing.

Lowe, L. (1996). *Immigrant acts: On Asian American cultural politics.* Durham, NC: Duke University Press.

Matsuda, M. (1995). Looking to the bottom: Critical legal studies and reparations. In K. Crenshaw, N. Gotanda, G. Peller, & K. Thomas (Eds.), *Critical race theory: The key writings that formed the movement* (pp. 63–79). New York, NY: The New Press.

McGuire, M. E. (2007). What happened to social studies? The disappearing curriculum. *Phi Delta Kappan, 88*(8), 620–624.

McLaren, P. (1997). *Revolutionary multiculturalism: Pedagogies of dissent for the new millennium.* Boulder, CO: Westview Press.

Museus, S. D. (2013). *Asian American students in higher education.* New York, NY: Routledge.

Myers, J. P. (2006). Rethinking the social studies curriculum in the context of globalization: Education for global citizenship in the US. *Theory and Research in Social Education, 34*(3), 370–394.

Ng, J.C., Lee, S.S., & Park, Y. (2007). Contesting the model minority and perpetual foreigner stereotype: A critical review of literature on Asian Americans in education. *Review of Research in Education, 31*, 95–130.

Nussbaum, M.C. (1996). Patriotism and cosmopolitanism. In M.C. Nussbaum & J. Cohen (Eds.), *For love of country: Debating the limits of patriotism* (pp. 2–20). Boston, MA: Beacon Press.

Obama, B. (2015, March 23). *FACT SHEET: President Obama announces over $240 million in new STEM commitments at the 2015 White House Science Fair.* Retrieved from https://www.whitehouse.gov/the-press-office/2015/03/23/fact-sheet-president-obama-announces-over-240-million-new-stem-commitmen

Passe, J. (2006). New challenges in elementary social studies. *The Social Studies, 97*(5), 189–192.

Rhee, J. (2006). Re/membering (to) shifting alignments: Korean women's transnational narratives in U.S. higher education. *International Journal of Qualitative Studies in Education, 19*(5), 595–615.

Romanowski, M.H. (2009). What you don't know can hurt you: Textbook omissions and 9/11. *The Clearing House, 82*, 290–296.

Rong, X.L. (2002). Teaching with differences and for differences: Reflections of a Chinese American teacher educator. In L. Vargas (Ed.), *Women faculty of color in the white classroom: Narratives on the pedagogical implications of teacher diversity* (pp. 125–144). New York, NY: Peter Lang.

Samimy, K.K. (2006). Multiple mentors in my career as a university faculty. In G. Li & G. Beckett (Eds.), *Strangers of the academy: Asian women scholars in higher education* (pp. 105–117). Sterling, VA: Stylus Publishing.

Schmidt, R. (2002). Racialization and language policy: The case of the U.S.A. *Multilingua, 21*(2/3), 141–161.

Schmidt, S.J. (2012). Am I a woman? The normalization of woman in US history. *Gender and Education, 24*(7), 707–724.

Shrake, E.K. (2006). Unmasking the self. In G. Li & G. Beckett (Eds.), *Strangers of the academy: Asian women scholars in higher education* (pp. 178–194). Sterling, VA: Stylus Publishing.

Sleeter, C.E., & Grant, C. (1991). Race, class, gender and disability in textbooks. In M. Apple & L. Christian-Smith (Eds.), *The politics of the textbook.* New York, NY: Routledge.

Sleeter, C.E., & Grant, C. (2003). *Making choices for multicultural education: Five approaches to race, class and gender.* New York, NY: Wiley.

Stanley, C.A. (2006). Coloring the academic landscape: Faculty of color breaking the silence in predominantly White colleges and universities. *American Educational Research Journal, 43*, 701–736.

Stanley, W.B. (2005). Social studies and the social order: Transmission or transformation? *Social Education, 69*(5), 282–286.

Takaki, R. (1988). Strangers from a different shore: A history of Asian Americans. Boston, MA: Little, Brown and Co.

Tuan, M. (1998). *Forever foreigners or honorary whites? The Asian ethnic experience today.* New Brunswick, NJ: Rutgers University Press.

Tyson, C. A., & Park, S. C. (2006). From theory to practice: Teaching for social justice. *Social Studies and the Young Learner, 19*(2), 23–25.

van Manen, M. (1990). *Researching lived experience: Human science for an action sensitive pedagogy.* Albany: State University of New York Press.

Wade, R. (2007). *Social studies for social justice: Teaching strategies for the elementary classroom.* New York, NY: Teachers College Press.

Westheimer, J. (2009). Should social studies be patriotic? *Social Education, 73*(7), 314–318.

Westheimer, J., & Kahne, J. (2004). What kind of citizen? The politics of educating for democracy. *American Educational Research Journal, 41*(2), 237–269.

Wu, F. (2002). *Yellow: Race in America beyond black and white.* New York, NY: Basic Books.

Zong, G. (2005). Road less traveled: An Asian woman immigrant faculty's experience practicing global pedagogy in American teacher education. In G. Li & G. Beckett (Eds.), *Strangers of the academy: Asian women scholars in higher education* (pp.105–117). Sterling, VA: Stylus Publishing.

Chapter 5

The Silencing of International Faculty

The Enemy Inside and Out

Paula Guerra

WHO I WAS AND WHO I WAS BECOMING

I was able to come to the United States as a master's graduate student with an Organization of American States (OAS) fellowship. It had been clear from the beginning that being a woman, who could teach mathematics, and speak English, had set me apart. I was what they were looking for, and they said I was also what they needed. I believed that story, and it made me confident in my ability to succeed in the United States. I was placed in the Southwest, which comforted me, as I knew there would be other Latin@ with whom to lean on. But interestingly enough, those Latinos were not in my program and I could barely find them in my college. Also, I did not see them at the university as faculty. They were there though, cleaning, serving, and fixing things. Although this did not provide the comfort I had envisioned, it did not discourage me. Instead, it made me cautious.

I was awarded a full scholarship for a Ph.D. program from an institution that wanted me to work on one of its research projects, which was an area of interest for me as well. At that time I started working in urban schools in the area primarily as a research assistant. However, additional tasks included teaching every once in a while, working with small groups of children, testing them, and providing professional development to the teachers. This experience, along with the research I was conducting in urban schools, helped me realize that the underfunded schools, with poor teacher attrition and which considered underachieving according to standardized test results, were urban schools and predominately populated by Latinos. I listened to the Latino school children's stories. I did so because they conversed with me in Spanish, something they were not allowed to do with their classroom teachers, not even those who were Latinos, because the school was located in an area

51

that was in the midst of legislation that would make it illegal to "teach" in any other language except English. I used the term *teach*, because the truth is using Spanish to teach had turned into something that teachers did not feel they could do, even if it could mean the difference between passing and failing for their young students.

The students told me about their memories of home, their families, their likes and dislikes, and how all of that was lost after moving to the United States. I remember a boy in the second grade telling me about his room in Mexico. "It was blue," he said. He had decorated it with pictures of fish, because he "liked fish." Naively, I asked about his room here. He told me: "No, I don't have a room here. I sleep in the living room with my brother." What was important for him, it seemed, had been lost, and the reasons why his family had moved may have not been enough to bring happiness to this young child. This is just one story, but there were many that sparked my interest in urban education, Latino students' success, English language learners, and social justice.

As I increased the knowledge of my area of interest, I learned more about Latino students. They were silenced in multiple ways, most profoundly by being denied the ability to speak in their native language. This was a form of censorship and racism (Houston & Kramarae, 1991). In a study of experiences of high school students conducted by Fine (1987), she found that "silencing constitutes a process of institutionalized policies and practices which obscure the very social, economic, and therefore experiential conditions of students' lives, and which expel from written, oral, and nonverbal expression substantive and critical talk about these conditions" (p. 157). I never imagined that just as the students in the schools I was visiting as part of the research study, and the students in Fine's study, I too would face similar conditions one day.

While working on the research project during my doctoral program, I could clearly see that the education the students were receiving was more of the banking type, that is, these students were considered to be empty vessels in which the teachers were to deposit knowledge (Freire, 2000). The knowledge that was transmitted was not of critical substance. Instead, it consisted of rules to be memorized and worksheets to be completed, lockstep, in the least amount of time possible. Even art consisted of a number of steps to be followed in sequence so that they all could re-create the same picture—all while they were under the pressure of responding to directions in a language that had yet to be mastered. Many of the students were bright, but teachers would not know because they could explain their thinking better in Spanish, than in English. I felt for them and their struggle. I thought I could do something for them; I failed to see that I was one of them.

I had never considered myself "a Latina" until I was labeled as such the minute I stepped on U.S. soil. Of course I knew I was in theory, since I spoke

Spanish. At times, it felt good to be grouped with the rest of Latin America. But in the end, it always led to me feeling as if we were so different, and I couldn't understand the constant lumping of all Spanish speakers into one group. At the same time, I was also convinced that I was White. There were some Afro descendants in Uruguay, and since I was not one of them; I felt that I could only be White. I was not blue-eyed-porcelain-doll White, but I still considered myself to be that of European heritage. That perception of my self ended the minute I stepped in the United States as I was forced to peel the White label off and replace it with the label of Latina. Yet, even when I was labeled as such, I still believed I was who I had thought I was for almost 30 years. That person had something in common with the children in those schools, but she also seemed to be different.

That difference made me believe I could be "the savior." I thought I could bring to others' attention the voices of the children and their families—the voices of young Latinas and their families, because I was, in part, one of them. I believed that I could lead the way because I had entered, I thought, a privilege circle through being a Ph.D. student in an important research institution in the States. In addition, I felt that I could lead because I had been privileged so I thought that I could make a change by being a role model and intermediary, helping Latinos voices be heard. However, I found that while I was not completely wrong, I missed a significant detail; even though my situation was not like that of the children and their families, I was also facing silencing and oppression.

THE FIRST TIME

As a graduate student, I had no role models in the predominantly White institution (PWI) at which I was studying. There was, for a time, one male Latino professor who eventually left, whose support could only do so much for me. Three out of the four members of my dissertation committee were men, two of whom were White, another member was a Latino, and the fourth member was a White woman. While I learned a great deal from all of them, it was difficult to have certain conversations with them. I had a hard time figuring out where the line was drawn about what was and was not appropriate to say and when I had to be politically correct about my dissertation topic (exploring the identities young Latinas develop while being successful at learning mathematics). I felt I had to be careful so as not to offend any of my committee members. There were a lot of conversations about oppression between me and the committee members. My participants felt oppressed by "the White man." I had a lot in common with my participants. "The White man" would also be part of the group who would ultimately approve (or not) my dissertation. It was hard, but for the most part I knew that I could achieve success.

I was able to resolve the fear of stepping on someone's toes and be honest with myself and write what I wanted to write because I realized the committee members were also interested in issues of social justice. Even though my professors did not grasp the concept some of the times because they had difficulty stepping away from theory and stepping into practice, they were open to hear me and support me for the most part. For example, some of the committee members found it acceptable to make jokes about some of the behaviors Korean graduate students (who also worked for the project I was working for) had about respect for elders and superiors, embarrassing them and making it harder to step away from those behaviors. I do not believe these committee members meant to do so, but the practice of equity and social justice is complex sometimes. Yet I was required to change the expression "White man" to "hegemonic discourse" in my dissertation. I was told "White man" was personally offensive to them and their families, so the term had to be changed. I complied because I felt I had no power, and after all it did not seem like a big deal. At the time, I did not realize that this was really not any different than not allowing students to speak Spanish in class.

And so it went, almost unnoticed, the first time that I was clearly silenced.

SILENCING CAN COME FROM ANY DIRECTION

Perhaps one reason my silencing went unnoticed was due to the fact that I persisted with my plans and my dreams. I eventually graduated and secured a position in another PWI located in the southeastern United States. The student population at the university where I was an assistant professor was 70 percent White and was comprised predominately of females; therefore, my classes were populated mostly by White females. The population of faculty and staff was also predominately White; thus, the students had limited experience with faculty of color and/or international faculty. I had learned about the struggles of new professors, but it seemed as if some new professors, many of whom were international faculty and faculty of color, struggled more with their teaching than others. The phenomenon of females of color facing resistance from their White students has been studied in the past (Skachkova, 2007; Stanley, 2006). It was not only I but also other faculty of color and other females of color would share my pain. However, being aware of this phenomenon did not make it any easier.

I remember in one class, students rolled their eyes at me—on the first day. It may seem like a small detail, and I took it as a way for them to cope with stress since they shared in their course introductions that it had been hard for them to learn mathematics and the thought of learning how to teach mathematics could be intimidating, as well. But the disrespect I subsequently saw in their eyes and their behavior was also because the one teaching the mathematics course was a woman and, even worse, a woman of color. Eventually, the rolling eyes turned into sarcastic answers, constant challenging of my statements, and unnecessary interruptions during class. When I called the disruptive students in for a meeting in my office, they refused and told me they would not show up. And that was that.

The students would not come to my office, nor would they talk to me. I never had the chance to tell them what I wanted to talk about, but I guess it was clear. For the second time I was silenced—this time by my students, and this time it did not go almost unnoticed—it was very apparent. It was evident they did not find my class interesting, but I thought that they would at least pretend they thought their professor had something important to tell them. Instead, they had no respect for my authority and disregarded anything I had to say to them. The behavior of my students led me to share the situation with my supervisor, which is a perfect segue into the next sequence in my story.

WHEN REMEDY IS WORSE THAN THE DISEASE

I met with my supervisor, who was a White male, to share the struggles I was experiencing with my students. I asked him for advice on how to respond to this situation because I wanted to believe this was not the first time something like this had happened. At that time, I did not know that he had already met with my students. It was not until days later when I found out that two of my students, both White females, met with him to complain about my teaching.

I listened as he told me that I was talking too much in the class about being culturally relevant and that I had to be "culturally relevant to my White students." He went on to say that I had to meet students where they were. Apparently this meant I needed to smile more frequently, because these were "sweet girls from the South." I did not believe this approach addressed the problem, but it was only the beginning; he had additional advice for me.

My supervisor proposed that on the first day of class I apologize for my accent and that I try and be more apologetic about my background being so different from my students. He stated that if I tried to appear to be more like the (White) group, the students would feel safer in my class. In other words, I could not be myself. The only issue, in his eyes, was that I was not like my students. I was told, in that meeting, that I had to become someone else.

This wasn't simply silencing me; this was a blatant attempt to erase my very being. It left me feeling angry and helpless. I had been silenced by my students, and in an attempt to reclaim my voice, I had been oppressed by my supervisor, who was clear about who had "privilege" within the department. His comments were covertly explicit in highlighting what I did not have—the privilege that comes with being White in the United States. Privilege was defined for me, and it was based on the dominant culture. My culture and funds of knowledge were dismissed much like those of the children described earlier in those urban schools in the Southwest. They were not valued. The expectation was that they should be eliminated from the equation if at all possible.

WHAT WE HEAR AND WHAT WE DO NOT SAY

I did not have the opportunity to say much nor was I given the opportunity to have my case heard. But I had the opportunity to hear things that would help me to navigate White-dominated academia. My supervisor telling me to be "culturally responsive to my White students" was only one example. "Equity shmequity" was another. This was a way to disregard equity in education by my boss when I was a research assistant. That same boss stated at a meeting in front of other professors and fellow research assistants that the fact I was offered multiple interviews (for academic positions) was because I was a Latina. All of these statements sent a message to me: my story was absolutely irrelevant and was not worth telling. From then on what mattered was where I was (the United States) and how I was supposed to behave as a result of the belief of others—act like a "Latina" as part of a minoritized group whose needs and truths come second to those of the dominant group. Perhaps I started to set my expectations based on the beliefs of others because this was not an isolated case. I heard similar statements, in different settings, many times. Or, perhaps I just started playing a game where I pretended I believed what others said about me. I did not believe they were right about those images they had about me, but I thought "letting it go" and "staying out of trouble" by not explaining myself and correcting their wrongness made my way easier. By pretending in this way and playing this game by their rules I began to silence myself.

The aforementioned examples came from different voices, but all of them were White males who were deemed to be successful and who had all reinforced that my experiences, voice, and achievements may not be recognized, with no clear explanation provided as to why that was the case. The statements, always delivered matter-of-factly, ended the conversation, and while there are other ways in which I have been silenced, these experiences, which happened when least expected and were delivered by individuals I felt would support me, were most disorienting.

While trying to develop different strategies to address the unhappiness I felt as a minoritized faculty member on campus, I heard about and was eventually invited to the "Black Caucus," a group of African American faculty who had experienced some of the same things that international faculty of color experienced. I found it hard to feel welcomed into a group that expressed clearly in their name whose interests they held. Not being American, or better said, not being from the United States, had been clearly a reason to separate faculty. International faculty who cannot call themselves "American" in the States (whether we are actually American or not) observe from the periphery how some of the conflicts start and are resolved without having much input in any of them. The "Black Caucus" was no different. I was reminded that I could tell my story, but it was secondary.

When the conversation about race and racism is focused only on the experiences of one group, then the other groups are also being silenced. This silencing included not only Latinas but also a number of Asian faculty employed at the university, who may have been treated as if their struggle with racism was not as important, or as if it did not exist at all, yet another way that I felt I was silenced. In some ways, this silencing felt worse because sometimes I was silenced by people who I thought to be allies and friends.

The struggle of finding a space for our voices to be heard among faculty in general and along with those of other faculty of color is one other international faculty and I have experienced. Working in the South with its racial history made this very clear for me. It was natural for me to adopt the struggles of African American faculty, as they were similar to mine, and fight against oppression, but I did not feel my commitment and support were reciprocated. It is natural to want our individual needs to be attended to first, but I believe that given our shared experiences and needs joining efforts would be the most efficient way to respond. That can happen only if all of those involved embrace the same ideal. That did not seem to happen; thus I found myself with no safety net or safe space in which to function. This is even worse when it seemed as if the media solely focus on the struggles African Americans face and barely mention the struggles that Latinos and others faced—we were forgotten and silenced. Also, when we chose to have an official faculty group address issues of equity, that group targeted only African Americans, so we had a problem. When the administration chose to address the same problems all faculty of color were facing by bringing speakers who targeted African Americans, we had a problem.

PROTECTING OURSELVES

It is interesting how some words get a whole different meaning in certain contexts. I had been told that my time as a junior faculty member was being "protected." In reality I was being denied an opportunity that not only I had been waiting for but for which I had spent a good amount of that time preparing. For example, I was denied a signature at the last moment, which I needed for a grant application and which I had sought and received support for previously. Suddenly, it was decided by my supervisor that dedicating my time to this grant and research was inappropriate. The ultimate decision as to the value of my work was denied to me, and I was not allowed to explore the viability of my project. This was decided for me, and my research interests, my knowledge on the topic, my will—none of it mattered. My agency was taken away, and that which was important to me, as an international faculty of color, would remain without analysis.

Here, like before, there was no worse "protection" than the one I was doing for myself as I did not speak up and challenge that decision. I was not doing this in isolation as there were more of us, international faculty and faculty of color, who were also "protecting ourselves." We denied ourselves the opportunity to study what we were interested in if it meant or could result in conflict with superiors and hoped for a next time while we made ourselves busy with someone else's research agenda. *Protection* was another word for *silence*.

We did not need to discuss exactly from what or whom we were supposed to be protected, but we needed to protect ourselves to reach the promised land of tenure. Sometimes that meant doing jobs we did not want to do, but this was normal. I observed some faculty giving in to the demands from some students, even though the demand was unreasonable and, in the end, would be to the detriment of the students' education. But, to avoid power struggles with students, some of my colleagues preferred to give in. This type of behavior tended to be at its worst when we removed ourselves from important conversations that happened within the department or the college, as a way to avoid confrontations that may cost us much later on. In these cases, we silenced ourselves.

Meetings of any kind tended to be difficult. The words from me and other international females of color had to be selected carefully. In general I, along with other faculty of color, considered a meeting "successful" if we left without "contributing" much. No one was specifically talking louder over our voice or disregarding what we said. We simply "chose" to be silent. As stated before, this was the worst kind of silencing because it was self-inflicted; we were cognizant in giving over the power that was ours to those in the dominant culture.

This kind of silencing indirectly puts us, faculty of color, in the ugly situation of not supporting each other. Conversations with other international faculty revealed the frustration and shame of not being able to "reply all" to an e-mail or comment back in a meeting, when it meant going against the dominant group in the college. When we did this, we did not support each other and in fact contributed to our marginalization.

There are also situations in which e-mails were sent to all faculty in the college, and heated debates took place in which international faculty rarely participated. It may have seemed as if I was not involved in the debates, and some may have wondered why I did not participate, but when contributions in the past had been judged solely based on one grammatical mistake, it was hard to want to reply at all much less to "reply all." It was difficult to engage in written form when in the hallways I had heard statements such as "cannot speak English," and I knew, or at least it felt like, they were whispering about me or about one of my fellow international faculty. These comments send a message to all of us who speak English as another language. When and how we say things is more important than what we say, which makes it difficult to put ourselves out there. This was yet another way that we were silenced, both externally and internally, and also shamed.

Another example of silencing took place during a poorly attended meeting. There were a majority of males in attendance who were not literate in issues of social justice and education. We were meeting to discuss student teaching placements abroad and expected candidate outcomes. Heated discussions took place during meeting, and voices were raised. At one point the discussion focused on the future of studying abroad in our college. The woman leading the meeting found it hard to find her own voice, as she was constantly interrupted and talked over. There were only two other women there—both of us were international faculty, and, in the end, we wished we had decided not to attend. Everyone there wanted our support, and our options were to either go against the two male faculty members, who were also members of the Tenure and Promotion Department Committee, or go against our own ideas. As I chose to say nothing, betraying myself, I came to understand better why the Latino teachers in the urban schools where I was a research assistant were not allowing their Latino students to speak Spanish in their classrooms, not even among themselves—it was likely because they were "protecting" themselves.

FAILING OURSELVES

We often think that once we are tenured, we will be given the opportunity to be less "protective" and reclaim our voice. But is that really true? For years we learned to remain quiet, dress up what we say so it is less "us" and more "them," and to do half of what we want and double what we do not believe in, which is what I believe they want. Can one really change that practice just because we received a paper saying we are now in a better category than what we used to be? Does this new title make us equal to White American faculty in a PWI? It is difficult to determine if such a space could be reclaimed when our voices have gone unheard for so long.

We failed ourselves in keeping silent. We burned bridges with those with whom we naturally wanted to connect. We did not support each other because we did not want to "get in trouble." We only privately shared that we agreed, but we warned others that if asked, we may have to at least stay out of the conversation. Our caution became a habit, and habits are sometimes hard to break.

We silence our opinions. We silence our knowledge. We silence our interests for research and teaching. We oppress ourselves, and we allow others to oppress us as well. We function under rules that we know are unfair, but we are so worried about the small picture, like a Third Year Review, or Tenure and Promotion, that we feel we cannot afford to go against those rules, at least not for now. Or maybe "not just now" is what we say to ourselves.

The ways, both big and small, in which we betray and silence ourselves, make us tired. Those ways that fail ourselves do not let us and those coming after us experience a different reality in academia. In my case, I often wonder what it would be like to leave academia. I compare myself with my fellow teachers back home, and it seems as if they have happier, full lives. But I love what I do! Or better, I love what I set myself to do some day—to not have to worry about all the politics and to look forward to the day when the colleagues with whom I want to work are able to pursue their interests, as I pursue interests of my own.

I am not placing the blame on international faculty of color. It is clear that the silencing we do is done as a response to the climate in the institution and does not reflect the ideals and morals of these faculty. If the climate in the institutions were more welcoming and accepting, then probably it would be easier to take risks. The influence White faculty have on us, international faculty, is immense. I have had as many chairs in my department as the years that I have been a faculty member of the said department (more than three). Unfortunately, none of those chairs have been of color and none of them have been international faculty. It is not that we are lacking smart, capable international faculty who could lead a department.

TO LIBERATE OURSELVES

The reason I highlighted the silencing we do to ourselves is that it is perhaps the first silence that should be broken. Freire (2000) professed that it is not the oppressor who can liberate the oppressed. It is the oppressed who not only will liberate themselves but who will give back their humanity to their former oppressors. The system may silence us, but it will not change itself. It is us who need to share our voice, find our space, and change the system.

The silence that is imposed on international faculty and that we impose on ourselves is not only stopping us from succeeding in what we love, but it also stops others, within White-dominated academia, to learn from our experiences and enrich their lives. To listen to us means for them to learn how to treat others with respect, understanding, and accepting of their culture.

I would like to believe that listening to me means to understand a more humane side to those children in the urban schools in the Southwest. It also means to understand their needs, what they miss, and who and what they love, and even to want to know their story. To see students in this way should help educators and teachers approach their education in a way that is not focused on "what is missing," but instead focused on "what they bring" and the story that needs to be told.

It is interesting to think that at my arrival, I thought my voice was not only valuable but also needed. That comfort and confidence rapidly declined. What I thought I was bringing, and others needed, was thought to be unnecessary and perhaps even an annoyance. Who I am and what I want to be do not seem to be taken seriously. What I then wanted to do, to make a change in the lives of many children living in the United States, became what seemed to be an almost impossible crusade. I became one of my subjects. And like my voice, I did not feel as if there was a space for my story to be told.

The voices of international faculty in academia are more relevant today than ever, and yet we face both the silencing from our environment and the condemnation for our silence. Some may believe that we are not committed—that we do not want to get involved. However, our reality is an overexperience of doors closing to our contributions. We are punished either way, so we are always punished, and when that sanction does not come from the outside, then it is us who inflict it upon ourselves. Although my experiences may not be the same experiences of all international faculty of color across the United States, it is the experience many others and I are having.

Perhaps, I can still complete the goal that I set for myself many years ago. It is a goal that will be impossible to reach, unless I find a way to break the imposition of silence coming from both inside and out. There are several barriers to break and walls to demolish, but perhaps if different minoritized groups can come together and find a common and more inclusive voice, then dominant groups would find it harder to avoid listening. Instead of marginalized groups focusing on who had been silenced the most or for a longer time, groups whose voices have not been heard, or groups who have yet to find their voice, must focus on an idea of community and highlight the things they have in common. A supportive community could informally, and formally as part of the institution, help everyone who is silenced to find the courage and space to talk.

62 *Paula Guerra*

REFERENCES

Fine, M. (1987). Silencing in public school. *Language Arts, 64*(2), 157–174.
Freire, P. (2000). *Pedagogy of the oppressed.* New York, NY: Bloomsbury Publishing.
Houston, M., & Kramarae, C. (1991). Speaking from silence: Methods of silencing and of resistance. *Discourse & Society, 2*(4), 387–399.
Skachkova, P. (2007). Academic careers of immigrant women professors in the US. *Higher Education, 53*(6), 697–738.
Stanley, C.A. (2006). Coloring the academic landscape: Faculty of color breaking the silence in predominantly White colleges and universities. *American Educational Research Journal, 43*(4), 701–736.

Chapter 6

Reframing Resistance

Steering into and through Student Resistance to Diversity Course Content

Michael D. Smith

AN ORIGIN STORY

In every family there are stories about you that practically beg to be told and retold. Often, these family stories communicate some embarrassing yet essential insight about the subject, and my family is no different. As an assistant professor who spends a significant portion of professional and personal energy reading, writing, and teaching about the intersections between race, power, privilege, and education, it seems fitting to begin this chapter with my earliest memory of Blackness serving as a social marker. As it is with most attempts to recall our earliest experiences, *actual* memories become entangled with *given* memories. The story about the experience bleeds into the recollection of the experience, effectively blurring the borders of each.

One of my mother's favorite stories about my racial awareness comes from my first day at school. I grew up in a small city in Central Virginia, in a place that our family has called home for multiple generations. In this city, the public school system left a lot to be desired, so my mom decided that I would go to the local private Catholic school—never mind that it was predominantly White and we were Southern Baptist. As the story goes, after coming home from school on the first day, my mom asked, "How many Black kids are in class with you?" To her surprise and amusement, I replied, "I don't know, but I'll ask Sister Mary Catherine tomorrow." Looking back at our first-grade class picture as an adult, it is clear that there were two other Black kids, and for the remainder of my school experience, I was always one of a small handful of Black students in the room. Thus began a complicated relationship with race and identity in predominantly White spaces.

At that point, I had not learned to conduct the "brown-people headcount" that I now often do unconsciously. Though I knew I was Black nominally, I did not have an understanding of what it meant existentially. While I matriculated through that school system, I learned implicitly and explicitly about the politics of race. To be clear, the formal and informal educational experiences were invaluable, and I remain friends—or at least *friendly*—with many of my childhood peers. Engagement with my peers provided access to intercultural frames of reference, cultural capital, and communication strategies that have served me well over the years. However, there were other aspects of the experience that were hard to reconcile as a child. For instance, it was hard to reconcile why and how some of my school friends could comfortably participate in Country Club functions that excluded Black people. It was hard to understand how dating at our school between a White boy and an Asian or Latina girl was permissible, but a relationship between a Black boy and White girl was socially constructed as "interracial" and thus socially problematic. It was hard to reconcile the backhanded compliment expressed to my mother by a White parent, "You know Michael is not like the rest of them" (referring to other Black boys).

At the same time I experienced the (un)spoken stigma concerning Blackness at school, the stigma of being White-by-proxy occurred in my engagement in predominantly Black spaces. Participating in cultural border crossing required recognizing and, sometimes, (re)adjusting to the contextual social demands of a simultaneously foreign and familiar environment. These semipermeable borders were demarcated by performances of identity (e.g., dress, speech, affinities, communication styles) that were socially constructed as normative and, therefore, acceptable. Black peers served as sentries at the gates, emboldened with the conferred capacity to stamp or reject my cultural passport. I remember bracing myself each time I was in a position to divulge that I went to the local private school knowing that such an admission marked me, putting my authentic Blackness on the table for examination, interrogation, and authentication. I remember vividly having my authentic Blackness questioned by my cousins' friends as they wondered aloud about the presence of the hard rock Guns N' Roses cassette sharing space in my carrying case alongside the hip-hop group Public Enemy. Like a baby bird returned to the nest bearing the stench of human hands, I *looked* like one of "us" but *felt* like one of "them."

From home, I received yet another (in)formal indoctrination about rules of engagement as a Black male. My mom had specific ideas about Black male presentation of self in hair, dress, speech, and conduct. This often presented in a cavalcade of nos.

- No, you cannot have an earring. I don't care if Michael Jordan has one. Michael Jordan doesn't have to interview for a job.
- No, you cannot embellish your high-top fade like hip-hop artists Kwamé the Boy Genius or Big Daddy Kane.

- No, you cannot open that in the store, and, while you're at it, don't forget to get a receipt and a bag for that gum.
- No, it's not funny or appropriate to answer the phone like J.J. from "Good Times."

Taken together, the formative experiences as an outsider–insider within predominantly White spaces and an insider–outsider in predominantly Black spaces combined to set the trajectory for how I reconciled my sense of racial identity. The racial consciousness that began in Virginia echoes into my personal and professional spheres years later. At this point, I have been teaching and studying race, racism, and education for approximately 15 years, including 8 years in my current position as a faculty member at a predominately White institution (PWI) in New York's Hudson Valley. I am one of two Black faculty members in the School of Education, and this (lack of) representation has its attendant complicating realities related to schoolwide conversations about diversity. To traverse the gauntlet leading to tenure and, ultimately, professional longevity in academe, faculty members must deftly balance the sometimes competing demands of service, scholarship, and teaching. The literature on the lived experiences of faculty of color in PWIs is replete with narratives articulating the relative costs to being an embodied other and conspicuously visible performer. My formative experiences in predominately White spaces and support within my most immediate professional setting (i.e., department and unit) may act as a partial inoculation against some of the potentially toxic elements experienced by other faculty of color in PWIs. I have had the good fortune of (in)formal faculty mentors who helped me to identify service that, to the degree possible, was meaningful yet manageable. I am situated in a department that understands my scholarship and values my contribution to the discourse. Placed within a different department or in the absence of mentorship my narrative would be very different.

My central orientation toward narratives and storytelling is filtered through the frame of phenomenology. Phenomenology demands attention to the conscious act of storytelling and the deeper meaning of the stories (un)told (Smith & Fowler, 2009). That is, given that we cannot tell *everything*, we find meaning in the *particular* narratives elevated into the storyteller's consciousness from the vast constellation of possibilities. The aspect of my professional life that feels most marked by real (and perceived) otherness, and thus the focus of my critical scholarly gaze broadly and this chapter specifically, is within the realm of teaching. Within this chapter, I will share insights gleaned from reflection on years of experience teaching about race and racism in a PWI. My current teaching rotation typically includes two courses where the intersection between race, power, privilege, and schooling share center stage.

I teach a graduate and undergraduate version of a course focusing on aspects of diversity and education. Broadly, I aim to unpack the central features of the ethos that I have developed to manage this terrain. Specifically, I will address lessons learned about negotiating student resistance to diversity course content in my (under)graduate courses. This includes an essential reframing of the resistance proffered by students, as well as recognizing when one should steer into and/or around said resistance.

UNDERSTANDING STUDENT RESISTANCE TO DIVERSITY

> Adults find it difficult to see the assumptions they hold about race as partial, fragmented, incomplete, or wrong because stories recounting racialized experiences are part of an individual's entire being, including emotions and imagination. Consequently, the knowledge individuals claim to possess about race often goes unquestioned. (Manglitz, Guy, & Merriweather, 2014, p. 113)

Like the possibility for scalding your mouth when biting into a fresh slice of pizza, student resistance is a hazard that comes with teaching about diversity in PWIs. My courses require all students to engage in critical inquiry about their racial identity and its relative impact on their lived experiences. However, according to the literature, this is a task for which many White students come to the course having little to no prior experience nor the requisite interpretive heuristics needed to make applications to their personal and professional experiences (Tatum, 1997). Further, because the lived experiences and consequences of race are rendered all but invisible for many White students, the current epoch provides scaffolding for underestimating the racialized experience of people of color. Though the explicit expression of racial intolerance has been sublimated, racial intolerance manifests in ways that are not always obvious to these students. McKinney (2003) notes that, compared to their progenitors, today's generation has very different founts of knowledge to draw from in the "construction of everyday whiteness"; that said, "White young people are also often less willing to express belief in stereotypes, due to social desirability bias, than were previous generations, and more concerned with presenting themselves as 'non-racist' " (p. 42). This presents a particular pedagogical predicament teaching to this population because contemporary White racism is more often characterized in "more subtle, covert or color-blind attitudes . . . than their parents or grandparents, who may have engaged in more overt and blatant hostility and discrimination" (McKinney, 2003, p. 42).

Over the years, managing students' resistance has been made easier by attending to the ways I frame and interpret their actions. Student resistance to diversity course content manifests in numerous ways. Schick and St. Denis (2003) note that "resistance to . . . anti-racist education manifests itself in many forms including various combinations of denial of inequality, selective perceptions of reality, guilt and anger, and at times withdrawal from learning" (p. 57). Smith and Tuck (2016) conceptualized resistance according to its active, passive, and actively passive features. Trent, Kea, and Oh (2008) referred to attempts to circumnavigate diversity course content as *distancing strategies*. In a similar investigation, Gay (2010) observed that her students:

> find consolation in silence, denial, and social disassociation; emphasizing aspects of diversity (such as gender, social class, and individuality) that are not as troublesome for them; separating themselves from any personal responsibility for causing and correcting oppressions and inequities; and concentrating on what should be to the exclusion of what is. (Gay, 2010, p. 146)

In their exploration of majoritarian stories, or dominant-culture narratives, Viesca, Torres, Barnatt, and Piazza (2013) identified color blindness, deficit-valuated diversity, and meritocracy as central themes of their White students' discourses on race (p. 101). Plainly, there are manifold psychological machinations available to help students salve cognitive dissonance in these contexts. Understanding the literature helps me to reframe its occurrence in my classroom. I am not the only one experiencing this resistance; it is a well-documented phenomenon experienced by many.

A well-timed act of active resistance or a seemingly coordinated display of (actively) passive aggression can even put seasoned instructors on their heels. In a compelling autoethnographic exploration of the entanglement experienced as the simultaneous message and messenger in a PWI, Amobi (2007) shared a poignant vignette about a student's active resistance in class. After explicitly discussing issues of racism in the class, a White student slammed his hand on the desk and expressed frustration with continued conversations about race. The author chose to capitulate and end the conversation but later asked in reflection:

> Should I just fold as I did in this scenario in order to deescalate dissent? Should I—like a seasoned airplane pilot—continue to gain altitude to ride above the storm? What message-delivery practices are useful for continuing to fly high in a stormy condition such as the one described in the scenario above? (p. 6)

My experience has resulted in a practice of choosing *consciously* and *proactively* to steer into or around such resistance.

STEERING INTO RESISTANCE

> First, a truly discursive space should be accommodating to resistance, ex-
> pressed [explicitly] or covertly. . . . Resistance to the flow of a conversation in
> a truly discursive space should itself become a subject of critique rather than
> a preemptive end to discourse. Secondly, every "truth" in a message tabled
> in a discursive space is subject to contention. . . . Helping students to attain
> a shift in their thinking about race and racism in education is a process, not a
> product. (Amobi, 2007, p. 7)

As a framework for understanding resistance, it has helped me to complicate and problematize the resistance that I experience. I have framed (and
reframed) student responses as my knowledge and experience deepen.
Resistance is not merely something that students are doing to me; it is far
more complicated and nuanced than that. I am not a victim of resistance
even if I am the de facto target by virtue of my position as the putative
class leader. Experience and mentorship has taught me that it is more fruitful to think about the functional utility of resistance for myself and my
students. That is, resistance is not given nor received in a vacuum; it has
functional meaning for the target and the object of the resistance. Like a
dog whistle that can only be heard by those whose ears are tuned to the frequency, I have learned to recognize resistance as something more textured.
Resistance is not necessarily an obstacle to my teaching or indictment of
my teaching quality; it is a transitory fact of the moment. Some forms of
resistance reveal more about the offenders' intercultural developmental
level related to the topic and course engagement demands (Bennett, 1993).
Sometimes, it is a signal that cognitive dissonance is in the process of
being reconciled—if inelegantly. At other times, I interpret it as a response
to being challenged to think about something in a way that may be more
cognitively, psychologically, and/or emotionally taxing than they are comfortable with at the moment.

Steering into resistance, then, is an approach to repurpose otherwise
destructive energy as a constructive good. If we look at the functional utility
of resistance holistically, it does not necessarily represent an end point for
students. Instead, resistance and discomfort may be productively viewed as
a stop along the path to insight (McHatton, Smith, Brown, & Curtis, 2013).
Actualizing this philosophy of steering into student resistance requires two
key components: designing for its inevitability while constructing course
infrastructure and deciding which areas are worth steering into. When I think
about the constructing course infrastructure, I account for the inevitable presence of resistance and build in response mechanisms.

Constructing Course Infrastructure

Despite the expectation of resistance, I believe that my teaching audience is essentially comprised of good, well-intentioned people. As such, I already know that the course content potentially problematizes their constructions of themselves as "good people." Further, the accompanying cognitive dissonance also presents the troublesome prospect of reconciling this construction with the course implying that they, indeed, (un)consciously engage in acts that are potentially homophobic, racist, and sexist, among other things, far more often than they know or would be willing to admit. An essential first step in this process is disabusing students of the notion that racism is enacted exclusively by preternaturally "bad people"—and the literature that we use bears this out in numerous ways.

In the contemporary U.S. culture, openly intolerant people generate headlines and derision; however, the behind-closed-doors intolerance is more likely to be that which is practiced and certainly experienced as more insidious. As McKinney (2003) notes, "Presumably, most 'average' whites would not align themselves with [heroes or villains]. Yet it is these average whites who are involved in everyday racism" (p. 39). Consequently, it makes more sense for me to acknowledge and bracket the acts of the "villains" in the beginning of the course and make the explicit focus of the course more so about our everyday (un)conscious intolerances. In so doing, the hope is to move the collective awareness from the realm of the unconscious to the conscious where behaviors may be more readily changed. In *Blindspots: Hidden Biases of Good People*, Banaji and Greenwald (2013) attempt to reveal the biases of people who otherwise "intend well and who strive to align their behavior with their intentions" (p. xv). However, even "good people" have internalized messages about the other that have coalesced into "blindspots." The sleight of hand here though is revealed as we understand that "hidden biases can influence our behavior toward members of particular social groups, [while] we remain oblivious to their influence" (Banaji & Greenwald, 2013, p. xii).

A central element in the course construction is the intense focus on cultivating the learning environment. For the most part, I allow a wide path into the discourse in my class. In general, I operate with a belief that the class can and should be a space where we have a community of learners who will engage ideas, share experiences, and draw experiential connections from the text to life. Counterbalancing that ideal is an assumption that putting this goal into practice talking about race and racism might also require us to wade into murky water and have conversations that might be uncomfortable. I trust the process that, if we can be relatively transparent and share our experiences and understanding of the material, by the course's end most people will leave with a deeper understanding than when they started. Consequently, when students stumble over what should be correct word usage (e.g., "Should it be 'Spanish' or 'Latino' or 'Hispanic'? I don't know what I should say.") or seem to second-guess themselves as they try to make a point, I encourage them to "Just say it." After all, the classroom is a space to learn and be corrected, when necessary. I acknowledge at the beginning of class that I don't have all of the answers and there may be times over the course of the semester when I'll "get it wrong" in the discussion of a topic. In fact, it's very likely that I will say something that will make some uncomfortable.

One of the biggest reasons I encourage such candor is that I would rather have students say aloud that thing that they would normally say privately so that it can be constructively examined, critiqued, explained, or clarified. Assuming that a student will stay engaged and not retreat into silence, such exchanges hold great potential to push a student "to clarify and defend some assertions that her silence [would have] prohibited her from understanding fully" (Ladson-Billings, 1996, p. 84). I actually prefer that they share a challenging belief or opinion in class where I can do the work of addressing it as opposed to having the conversation on the way to the cafeteria after class without the opportunity to explore, engage, and redirect together as a group. In a way, I hope that engaging and disagreeing in this way models for them how we participate in dialogues where we (sometimes strongly) disagree with others yet discuss our points of contention civilly.

With the door open for more types of narratives and connections to course material, we can also deconstruct and challenge beliefs that are grounded in shaky logic or unreliable sources. In Singleton and Linton's (2006) chapter on engaging in courageous conversations on race, the authors asked readers to consider the things they (a) don't know, (b) don't know they don't know, (c) don't know but think they know, and (d) know they know about race. Reading this text in the beginning of the course provides us with a dialogic shortcut later in the course when we encounter beliefs that are in some ways troublesome. To the student, we might ask "Is this belief about X, something you know you know, or something that you don't know but think you know?" or "When you say, 'They say X about Y group,' how reliable are 'they'? How confident are you in what 'they' 'know'?" What begins as a bit of an intellectual and existential knot (i.e., "Professor, how can we ever know that we know?") ends up being a useful way of thinking about the sources of knowledge that have informed our beliefs.

Sometimes taking this approach to class discussions about race can be problematic. There have been moments when allowing students to openly share opinions, perspectives, and experiences led to some uncomfortable conversations. A conversation on a reading about the achievement gap might turn unexpectedly and include students wondering aloud about why "these people of color cannot pull themselves up by their bootstraps" like their great-grandparents did when they emigrated from Europe. A conversation about White privilege may veer off into White students passionately discussing their perceptions of affirmative action as "reverse racism." Of course, I can handle these comments and offer cogent, well-considered replies, but I have to admit that sometimes it gets tense. Though I have invited the candor in their interpretations and responses to the readings, sometimes hearing their truths cuts a little close to the bone. In those more vulnerable moments it can be more challenging to bracket the personal hurt in order to respond professionally. This active negotiation of the tension between feeling (even marginally) offended personally but needing to find a professionally appropriate way to engage a student recalls Sue and his coauthors' (2007) discussion of the dilemmas inherent in responding to racial microaggressions. They state:

> [R]esponding with anger . . . (perhaps a normal and healthy reaction) is likely to engender negative consequences for persons of color as well. They are likely to be accused of being racially oversensitive or paranoid or told that their emotional outbursts confirm stereotypes about minorities. In the case of Black males, for example, protesting may lend credence to the belief that they are hostile, angry, impulsive, and prone to violence (Jones 1997) . . . [W]hile the person of color may feel better in the immediate moment by relieving pent-up emotions, the reality is that the general situation has not changed. (Sue et al., 2007, p. 279)

Understanding this, negotiating my own anxieties about students' interpretations of my responses (i.e., how will my status as a young Black man influence how they interpret and respond to my comments?) and possible reprisal on teaching evaluations (i.e., will I be experienced as a professor who encouraged multiple viewpoints or inhibited free expression?) factor into the real-time decisions that have to be made about how to construct responses that offer a truth that can be heard.

The Leonardo and Porter (2010) article, "Pedagogy of Fear: Toward a Fanonian Theory of 'Safety' in Race Dialogue," has been particularly influential in (re)consideration of the collateral damage that might occur as students of color get hurt by their proximity to these conversations. After all, they are not professionals paid to facilitate or participate in these conversations. They may not be ready nor willing to participate in conversations where their White peers reveal the (un)consciously racist beliefs that underscore their lived experiences. I know I can handle these exchanges when they happen, but I wonder, in hindsight, if I made the classroom unnecessarily uncomfortable. Leonardo and Porter (2010) believe that "in mixed racial company, race dialogue is almost never for the benefit of people of color and race-conscious whites" and "many students of color who seek 'safe' race discussions in public rarely find them, having to settle for the reality that most pedagogical situations involving race are violent to them" (p. 149). Establishing the parameters of safety also includes the potential for collateral damage. It is possible that my approach to democratizing discourse might also hold the potential for creating opportunities for harm. However, in my course evaluations, I rarely (if ever) have students remark that they felt as if they could not be heard if they disagreed with me, felt stifled in any way when they wanted to express what was on their minds, or felt personally threatened or invalidated during a discussion.

I program for resistance in the design of assignments as well. I have created multiple assignments that ask students to explore their beliefs and assumptions about the other. One of the newest additions to my assignment rotation came about as a direct response to persistent student resistance to the idea of implementing culturally responsive pedagogy (CRP) in their classrooms. Over a few semesters, students were routinely stating that CRP sounded good, but their anxieties about reactions to its implementation were reason enough to not bridge the theory-to-practice divide. As a result, I created an assignment that contained a thought experiment: students are asked to reflect on two to three aspects of implementing CRP in the classroom, discuss their anxieties around it, and then brainstorm ways to address these concerns within their setting. In so doing, the resistance and fear is made plain in their writing and becomes the subject of analysis. Concurrently, as an instructor, I am able to provide direct, focused, individual feedback that I hope addresses the concerns and makes the gulf between theory and practice appear more easily traversable.

Steering into Resistance Selectively

Through a set of rhetorical devices, course materials and activities, and assignments, the aim is to cumulatively nudge students to interrogate and complicate the worldview that they brought into the course. Causey, Thomas, and Armento (2000) refer to this process as *radical restructuring*. Within teacher education, radical restructuring leads to the "discovery of new paradigms, identification of new core concepts, and/or the creation of new schematic structures. Stated differently, dramatic changes or reorganization of one's belief structure can be viewed as a radical restructuring of one's world view" (p. 34). That said, it would be unwise and unrealistic to attempt to participate in this form of engagement with every student and at every instance of resistance. In my classes, reflection-in-action leads me to address resistance in large and small ways and a wide range of topics (Schön, 1983).

In PWIs, however, it seems that students' constructions of color blindness and understandings of active/passive (anti)racism are clear entry points to the discourse that must be addressed directly.

Color blindness

> The self-infliction of blindness to race, resistance to seeing, suggests that there is an ongoing series of decision points for White people when it comes to race. We are afforded the privilege to see or not to see as it suits us. Sometimes we choose the safer path and keep our blinders on. At other times, we risk seeing and leave ourselves exposed to the inequities around us. (Gordon, 2005, pp. 139–140)

I, too, experience the profession of not-seeing race as an active choice as opposed to a passive condition. That is, given the sociohistorical circumstances involved with the macro-narrative of race in the United States, it seems improbable (if not impossible) for an individual to "not see" race in interpersonal interactions. The cycle of socialization is so persistent and pervasive in the communication of ideas about race that color blindness seems, at best, disingenuine or emblematic of an unnuanced understanding of the function of race in contemporary U.S. culture. At worst, professions of color blindness are dishonest and emblematic of a willed optical delusion. By contrast, Winans (2010) offers an alternate interpretation of majoritarian color blindness narratives. She posits that color-blind narratives reveal less of an active obfuscation of inner beliefs and more so a White student's expression of the ideal toward which he or she strives. Specifically, she speculates about the possibility that when White students' claim that "they see beyond race, treat everybody the same, and thus define themselves as color-blind, they are seeking to define themselves as good moral people in an environment in which direct interaction with people of other races is limited" (p. 478). That is, Winans challenges teacher educators to contextualize the racialized discourse of White students such that one considers the degree to which expressed opinions are reflective of actual direct experiences or extrapolations based on broader cultural meta-narratives about the other. In the absence of direct experience with the other, received wisdom from cultural narratives is often accepted as a memetic substitute (Thomson, 1997). Winans (2010) cautions us to "consider the extent to which *what* students know and believe about race is bound up with *how* they know and learn" (p. 478).

As a teacher educator there is a responsibility though to interrupt this narrative and challenge teacher candidates to complicate, clarify, and refine their interpretive lens in this regard. Gordon (2005) advocates directly addressing color blindness lest one contributes to personal complicity or the complicity of our teacher candidates to move forward with potentially harmful uncritical habits of mind related to race. She acknowledges that "the work ahead is by necessity arduous and uncomfortable, in that it requires that we reveal our assumptions, and acknowledge and work against our privilege, so that we can give to others the real chances they deserve not merely to succeed in the system in which we might fail" (p. 147). I cannot in good conscience let these invocations of color blindness rest when they are spoken in class.

After semesters of responding to these notions in lectures and papers, I decided to anticipate it and proactively plan for it in the course design. Now, as a way to short-circuit the expression of the ideology before it gains purchase as a viable avenue of discourse, I provide readings featuring authors who challenge and critique this notion in the beginning of the course. This way, the ideology that was previously an impediment to students getting real with me, each other, and, most important, themselves has been complicated, addressed, and/or removed. Using readings as a lever in which to adjust the conversation also puts the troublesome construct in the center of the frame in class discussion. We can examine multiple sides of the argument from a simultaneously personal and impersonal perspective. With this small adjustment, my students and I are not put into opposition with each other debating the issue. Instead, we are standing figuratively around the discursive circle observing and engaging the textual arguments. I can frame my opinions around the text and collectively we can talk about aspects that we (dis)agree with and the accompanying reasons.

Active versus Passive (Anti)racism (i.e., Intent versus Outcome)

Each semester that I use Chapter 2 of Beverly Tatum's (1997) book *Why Are the Black Kids Sitting Together in the Cafeteria*, I can expect to receive resistance to an unspoken—but no less felt—principle found in her text. In her book, she presents the ideas of active racism, passive racism, and active antiracism through the metaphor of an invisible conveyor belt (p. 11). In her text, a conveyor belt represents the culture's momentum toward participating in the culture in ways that reify oppressive social relations. In an attempt to extend the metaphor, a person who is actively racist walks in the direction of the conveyor belt's momentum. A person who is passively racist stands still on the conveyor belt but eventually finds himself or herself in the same position as the active racist though without the same expressed intent and energy. To be antiracist, one must turn around and walk in the other direction. Look again, at the metaphor and see if you can see what's missing—the passive antiracist.

Many of my students would like to believe that not-acting is a neutral act and one can somehow not-act yet also not be implicated in a racist outcome. As an exercise, it is interesting to present the idea and let the students play with the permutations of the model that they might lead to a valid passive antiracist conclusion. That is, they would like to believe that their actions are neutral and it is my contention that they are not. Tatum uses an elegant metaphor that essentially suggests that one's intent does not matter as much as the outcome. Though it was not the explicit intent to end in a racist place, complacency eventuates in the same destination. Many students have developed a sense of a "nonracist" self that simultaneously allows for inaction and innocence, and Tatum complicates this idea considerably. I want students to feel compelled to act on behalf of the other, but simply telling them this still allows for the feeling of "at least I'm not doing harm" to maintain a whole sense of self. This text and exercise confronts this ego defense obliquely yet somehow directly. Students, in wrestling to defend their innocence, are tangled in their complicity. Instead of impassioned rallying cries to act (which I still find myself doing sometimes), it seems more effective to use a Socratic approach to facilitate or reverse engineer their arrival at the same location on their own.

STEERING AROUND RESISTANCE

As I became more comfortable with my professional identity and gained more experience, I realized that some resistance from students simply needed to be steered around instead of entertained. When I think about the process of steering around resistance, I define it as a psychological defense mechanism through which I maintain my confidence in my professional training and scholarship amid challenging circumstances. That is, the training serves as a pedagogical North Star that reliably guides my pedagogical approaches and helps me to manage student resistance to otherwise reasonable—yet challenging—instructional demands. Again, Amobi's (2007) aforementioned article is instructive. I can relate to and sympathize with an instructor who is attempting to engage students in a more critical conversation about race and has seriously second-guessed himself in the moment; I know the feeling intimately. I can distinctly remember picking out articles that I found interesting for a class, designing evocative open-ended small group discussion questions, and finding that they simply did not work in the class. The students, almost as if they decided beforehand to stage a coup d'état, were wholly unresponsive. In those moments, I too felt panicked and wanted to hit the ejector seat button to remove myself (or those stubborn students) from the class. I have wanted to end a class early, call a break to regroup, or just move on to another topic. I have actively hated teaching certain sections and dreaded going to the class to teach a particular group, yet had to muster the energy to fulfill my professional obligation. However, experience and trusting the process that I have designed for the course has taught me that this premature capitulation ultimately forecloses students' opportunities to learn even as it relieves me of the anxiety in the moment. Experience and discernment dictate the development of a counterintuitive comfort in the discomfort. Silence is uncomfortable, but it is not deadly. Sometimes it is useful to let a question hang in the air. At other times, it might be useful to name the silence enacted and then examine its presence (and what it is communicating).

Discernment also teaches us to distinguish what students cannot do from what they don't want to do. In the beginning of my career, I heard many student complaints about content or assignments as an indictment of my ability and/or pedagogical choices. That is, if they complained about a reading, it was my fault for picking things that were above their level—and to be fair, sometimes there was validity in that assessment. If they complained about an assignment, I perceived it as a failure on my part to design an assignment that related well to the course content or else was poorly designed. In my classes now, I still take in their feedback, but I attempt to separate their can'ts from their won'ts. For instance, a reading that people have complained about being too difficult might be made more accessible by pre-reading scaffolding. When students are provided with the proper scaffolding, later complaints about the reading seem to be more about an unwillingness to be challenged intellectually instead of the reading *actually* being too hard. In this instance, this resistance should be steered around instead of entertained meaningfully. I have met them at least halfway, and it is their job to do the intellectual work of an (under)graduate student. I have several papers in my courses that ask students to delve into their personal histories and explore aspects of their cultural identities, schooling experiences, and/or beliefs and assumptions about the other. Most of these assignments are written in an open-ended manner that allow for creative and personal approaches to addressing the requirements. Over time, I recognized that the open-ended aspects of the assignment may be great for some learners and awful for others, so I built in some scaffolding to provide a framework that provides a broad structure to compose the paper. That said, when resistance about constructing the paper is offered, I know that I have met them at least halfway. I steer around this resistance with my own resistance. I resist the temptation to create a prescriptive assignment that appeases students discomfort when experience has taught me that figuring out a way to construct the paper is part of the process.

I do not suggest that this approach to reframing resistance will be easy for everyone; however, this is an approach that has worked for me. This is a personal philosophy for simultaneously neutralizing and metabolizing that which might be experienced negatively and choosing to compel it toward a positive end. Working in this area over time, conversations with mentors and trusted others, and continued study have produced the callouses in many of the places needed to be effective in my teaching. By and large, my teaching evaluations have been positive. Students experience my classes as engaging and thought-provoking; and I have learned not to live and die by evaluations I get at the end of the semester. It is comforting to remember that I am not as good as my best evaluation nor as bad as my worst; a grain of salt should be taken with all feedback. Further, though student feedback is important, I cannot let (under)graduate students dictate what is done in the class when I have based my pedagogical decisions on defensibly sound training, scholarship, and principles.

Of course, this has implications for the tenure and promotion process. As an untenured faculty member you are particularly vulnerable. In fact, committing this to print is simultaneously an act of equal parts vulnerability, trust, and bravery from my own station as an untenured faculty member. In most spaces, the tenure and promotion process feels so opaque that one can understandably get caught in a feedback loop capitulating to the whims of students under his or her charge. The fear of unsatisfactory student evaluations of instruction could make you bend in ways that betray your training and pedagogical principles. As I have noted, resistance can feel like an indictment of your ability and worth. For this reason, it is even more important for faculty of color in PWIs to develop strategies for steering into and around resistance—perhaps faster than their White counterparts. In fact, this might be *especially* true for individuals who teach courses that have race, power, and oppression at its center. The literature reflects the reality that faculty of color—particularly those who teach these courses—often receive harsher student evaluations of instruction and consequently receive what might be experienced as "non-standard" scrutiny in the tenure and promotion process (Atwater, Butler, Freeman, & Carlton Parsons, 2013; Stanley, 2006).

Early in my teaching career I was fortunate enough to co-teach an undergraduate diversity course with my mentor (a gray-haired, White senior faculty member). While processing the course meetings we often talked about how students likely heard things differently from each of us individually and the possible value added by teaching together. It was actually affirming to hear an acknowledgment that race likely mattered and the message–messenger dynamic was not a figment of my imagination. Working with him over the course of multiple semesters helped me to hone an approach to cross-cultural communication that began in Virginia and continued to bear fruit in my professional endeavors.

I recognize how, when, and why to code-switch in a way that feels simultaneously appropriate and authentic. My presentation of self includes a tension between my authentic expression of self and a nod toward professional standards of decorum; yet I know presentation matters in ways that are deeply personal and political. Years ago, when I had dreadlocks, I had a conversation with my grandmother that both shook me and gave me grist for reflection. Concerned about how students and colleagues would experience me and evaluate my ability, she asked, "How are you teaching people's children with your hair like that?" The defiant part of me was incensed, but another part of me heard her concern. She did not want the message to get lost in the messenger. For faculty of color, this is a reality that must be acknowledged; presentations of self visually, aurally, and so on end up as part of the holistic experience of existence in PWIs. A White colleague who teaches the same course in a direct, in-your-face manner might be lauded for his or her directness. A similar approach from me might be experienced as defensive and aggressive. Survival dictates that I manage this accordingly. As such, I am practiced at telling a truth that people can hear and using Socratic teaching methods to help individuals arrive at their own answers—even if I have reverse engineered their path.

It is not unusual for students to ask for a prescriptive set of shortcuts for teaching from this perspective. While I provide them with some suggestions, I place more emphasis on developing the habits of mind of a culturally responsive educator. Using my teaching as an example, I tell them that the very approaches, assignments, and examples that worked last semester may indeed fall flat this semester if I took a reductionist approach to teaching. Instead, it seems more fruitful to enact the habits of mind to respond to the learning needs of the students who are actually in the room. Will this approach eventually lead to the tenure and promotion or reveal the flawed assumptions of a naive idealist? Honestly, I do not know. I go up for tenure soon, but I remain hopeful. More than anything, this is an approach to managing self, PWIs, and student resistance that feels right and true. I can feel at peace with the way that I have conducted myself, treated students, and honored my training—and at the end of the day, that feels like enough.

REFERENCES

Amobi, F.A. (2007). The message or the messenger: Reflection on the volatility of evoking novice teachers' courageous conversations on race. *Multicultural Education, 14*(3), 2–7.

Atwater, M. M., Butler, M. B., Freeman, T. B., & Carlton Parsons, E. R. (2013). An examination of black science teacher educators' experiences with multicultural education, equity, and social justice. *Journal of Science Teacher Education, 24,* 1293–1313.

Banaji, M. R., & Greenwald, A. G. (2013). *Blindspot: Hidden biases of good people.* New York, NY: Delacorte Press.

Bennett, M. J. (1993). Towards ethnorelativism: A developmental model of intercultural sensitivity. In R. M. Paige (Ed.), *Education for the intercultural experience* (2nd ed.). Yarmouth, ME: Intercultural Press.

Causey, V. E., Thomas, C. D., & Armento, B. J. (2000). Cultural diversity is basically a foreign term to me: The challenges of diversity for preservice teacher education. *Teaching and Teacher Education, 16*(1), 33–45.

Gay, G. (2010). Acting on beliefs in teacher education for cultural diversity. *Journal of Teacher Education, 61*(1–2), 143–152.

Gordon, J. (2005). Inadvertent complicity: Colorblindness in teacher education. *Educational Studies, 38*(2), 135–153.

Ladson-Billings, G. (1996). Silences as weapons: Challenges of a Black professor teaching White students. *Theory into Practice, 35*(2), 79–85.

Leonardo, Z., & Porter, R. K. (2010). Pedagogy of fear: Toward a Fanonian theory of "safety" in race dialogue. *Race Ethnicity and Education, 13*(2), 139–157.

Manglitz, E., Guy, T. C., & Merriweather, L. R. (2014). Knowledge and emotions in cross-racial dialogues: Challenges and opportunities for adult educators committed to racial justice in educational settings. *Adult Learning, 25*(3), 111–118.

McHatton, P. A., Smith, M., Brown, K. H., & Curtis, J. (2013). "First, do no harm": Purposeful preparation of culturally competent educators. *Multiple Voices for Ethnically Diverse Exceptional Learners, 13*(2), 19–31.

McKinney, K. D. (2003). "I feel 'Whiteness' when I hear people blaming Whites": Whiteness as cultural victimization. *Race and Society, 6*(1), 39–55.

Schick, C., & St. Denis, V. (2003). What makes anti-racist pedagogy in teacher education difficult? Three popular ideological assumptions. *Alberta Journal of Educational Research, 49*(1), 55–69.

Schön, D. A. (1983). *The reflective practitioner: How professionals think in action.* New York, NY: Basic Books.

Singleton, G. E., & Linton, C. (2006). *Courageous conversations about race: A field guide for achieving equity in schools.* Thousand Oaks, CA: Corwin Press.

Smith, M. D., & Fowler, K. (2009). Chapter 9: Phenomenological research. In J. Paul, J. Kleinhammer-Tramill, & K. Fowler (Eds.), *Qualitative research methods in special education.* Denver, CO: Love Publishing Company.

Smith, M. D., & Tuck, E. (2016). Decentering Whiteness as normal: Teaching about race in predominately White institutions. In S. Willie-Briton (Ed.), *Transforming the Academy: Faculty Perspectives on Diversity and Pedagogy.* NJ: Rutgers University Press, 13–36.

Stanley, C. A. (2006). Coloring the academic landscape: Faculty of color breaking the silence in predominantly White colleges and universities. *American Educational Research Journal, 43*(4), 701–736.

Sue, D. W., Capodilupo, C. M., Torino, G. C., Bucceri, J. M., Holder, A., Nadal, K. L., & Esquilin, M. (2007). Racial microaggressions in everyday life: Implications for clinical practice. *American Psychologist, 62*(4), 271.

Tatum, B. D. (1997). *"Why are all the Black kids sitting together in the cafeteria?":* And other conversations about race. New York, NY: Basic Books.

Thomson, R. G. (1997). *Extraordinary bodies: Figuring physical disability in American culture and literature.* New York, NY: Columbia University Press.

Trent, S. C., Kea, C. D., & Oh, K. (2008). Preparing preservice educators for cultural diversity: How far have we come?. *Exceptional Children, 74*(3), 328–350.

Viesca, K. M., Torres, A. S., Barnatt, J., & Piazza, P. (2013). When claiming to teach for social justice is not enough: Majoritarian stories of race, difference, and meritocracy. *Berkeley Review of Education, 4*(1), 97–122.

Winans, A. E. (2010). Cultivating racial literacy in white, segregated settings: Emotions as site of ethical engagement and inquiry. *Curriculum Inquiry, 40*(3), 475–491.

Chapter 7

A Lighthouse on the Shore and the Challenge of Trying to Shine

Ursula Thomas

It must begin with the lighthouse. According to maritime literature, a lighthouse is a tower with a bright light at the top located at an important or precarious place regarding navigation or travel over water. The two principal purposes of a lighthouse are to perform as a navigation support and also to caution boats similar to a traffic light or signal on the ocean or the sea (U.S. Government Printing Office, 1916). It is by no accident that I have chosen this image, this mental picture, to illustrate my function and existence in academia.

A Lighthouse on the Shore
I was created to be built, to shine with the light of ancestors' past buried in my soul,
A light not dimmed by slave ships with rarely seen hull but to dance,
The blueprint of my light, ages old, waiting to be unpacked, reworked, not worrying about what
is required only how, not worried about what danger is at the helm.
With my lighthouse built, I commanded the best from myself, ready to light my lamp.
The many attempts to ignite not expected but still, I light in spite of the storms and washouts,
Head held high despite the breakers and storms and committed to reignite the light, anxious but
confident, ready to engage the few reserves stored in my faith.
Sabotage is not gentle nor kind, but cunning like a siren.
When all my efforts are not enough to be sustained on this shore, should I choose another?
Is my light purely effervescent enough to carry away as I move away from this rocky
unforgiving place?

The waters answer, saying my light is enough and there is enough to start again, reignited bigger,
better, bolder, more brash and unapologetic.
Righteously, righteously indignant. (Thomas, 2015 self-published)

HOW DID I GET HERE (WASHING UP ON SHORE)?

Education as a Legacy

The legacy of education was passed down to me, and it will be the legacy that I will leave. I make the third generation of educators in my family. Education for Blacks, especially in the South, was an intentional gateway to civil rights, social justice, and the middle class. This was no different for my family coming from the Deep South. As I engaged in the generational work of education, racism was embedded in my DNA: I could see it, smell it, taste it, feel it, and read it. As a child, I was trained to detect it like a bloodhound. I now realize that this was a safety mechanism and a survival tactic. The detection of racism was as important as learning to read, write, and speak in the "King's English."

Racism along the Way

Racism along the way is expected, as it is as consistent as the tide coming in. My undergraduate collegiate experience at a historically Black university actually laid the foundation for social justice, cultural awareness, and resistance—which would later serve as my spiritual infrastructure. My graduate careers at two major research institutions that were predominantly White definitely exposed me to the cobblestones of racism that would eventually litter my pathway. As a student at my previous predominantly White institution (PWI), I experienced subtle and not-so-subtle microaggressions. Constantine and Sue (2007) define microaggressions as one of the "everyday insults, indignities and demeaning messages sent to people of color by well-intentioned White people who are unaware of the hidden messages being sent to them." An example of the subtle aggressions I experienced as a student would include being evaluated by criteria other than what was in the project rubric *after* I had a meeting with a White professor. Another instance of microaggression that I experienced would be the time when I and the only other Black student in the class were asked if Title I funding was or was not useful for students at predominantly Black elementary schools. As the only Black people in the class of 22 students, the professor, who was White, expected an answer on demand in front of all of our classmates as if we spoke for all people of color.

As an adjunct instructor at a historically Black college, I also learned information that was of great value. It was a valuable experience because I was hired by a White dean who knew I was in a doctoral program but also felt that I should be groomed for higher education. This dean also talked to me about the lack of women of color in higher education and shared that I had the disposition and passion for academics after observing me in his qualitative research courses.

As I moved from doctoral student to higher education faculty, I learned that support for my transition would come from both expected and unexpected places. On one hand, I received support from White males as allies, such as the dean mentioned previously, while on the other hand I experienced negativity from other women when support with regard to classroom discourse during graduate work was needed. Nonetheless, all of my experiences helped shape my career. Therefore, by the time I arrived at my third PWI in my higher education career, I had an idea of what to expect, or so I thought. I had both positive and negative experiences prior to this position, and they fed into the fact that no matter what the situation, I expected to have to prove myself and to be judged based on terms that may not always appear transparent or obvious. I had experienced some racial microaggressions at the previous PWIs, so I expected to have the same experiences at my third position—I knew that it came with the territory. What was different, however, was that it was my intention to stay at the third institution long term, which was different from my intention at my previous PWIs as a full-time faculty member. In my mind, I was prepared.

I AM HERE AND LOOK WHAT I BROUGHT

Setting Up Camp

I had been employed full time at two PWIs prior to this one. Upon completion of my doctoral program, I was hired as an assistant professor and utilized my experiences as a kindergarten teacher. The second position was an administrative position and, similar to the first position, came with a ranking of assistant professor in early childhood. Both hires were at regional institutions with evening programs designed for working adults. However, I was optimistic about this third position because it was more traditional than the other two professorial positions, and I was able to work with more traditional students, which I desired. Although I had been able to present at many conferences in my previous two positions, I looked forward to more time for research and writing with my third position.

I had the best-laid plans for my career at this institution. I had specific intentions to include my budding research agenda, which included the inter-disciplinary study of early childhood education, teacher dispositions, and social justice. I had the benefit of being a generalist who wrote from the consistent theme of diversity and disposition. I really wanted to focus on col-laborating with other departments and disciplines. I was interested in working to identify and promote practices and policies that create strong and closely coordinated partnerships and collaborations between other departments and programs associated with the educator preparation program and the univer-sity. In other words, I was interested in the "bridgework" that would build my qualitative research muscles. My intentions were to write and publish, alone and with others, since I had been told that collaboration was important to the university and the department. In order to be proactive in my quest for tenure, I created a chronological framework, semester by semester, year by year, based on the tenure and promotion handbook and feedback from annual evaluations. I actually made a list to monitor my accomplishments, and so it began.

INFRASTRUCTURE

Building My Lighthouse

As I set out to build my place at this third university, I had to understand the infrastructure if I was going to fit in. I needed to know the vision and the ideology of the leadership at the helm of the college's mission in order to better align myself with the leadership and, ultimately, for them to better align with me.

I sought guidance from someone who existed in the structure of power at the university, the University Provost. As I prepared to attend the new faculty orientation, I wrote down my burning questions, as I intended to get them answered as a part of my plan for success. That morning, I walked into the venue and surveyed the seating. I eventually chose a seat up front so as not to be ignored or hidden in plain sight. The provost introduced himself, gave his speech, and then proceeded to take questions. I waited patiently, and after many other questions, I got the chance to ask mine. I asked him what programs and strategies the university employed to retain faculty of color. This question was important to me because the institution was comprised of approximately 7 percent of the faculty who were culturally and linguistically diverse, so I was outdone when he responded, "The same thing we do for everyone else." He did not stutter, blink, or flinch. Even the White female who sat next to me was surprised at his response, as it did not seem that his statement was reflective of inclusiveness and nurturing diversity at the university. That response would inevitably haunt me for the entire time I was at the institution. I would later learn that his words would in some way be reflective of my experiences and ultimate departure from the university.

My first department chair at this institution paired me with a Black woman as my mentor, and although my sense was that this was done simply based on race it ultimately worked in my favor. My mentor and I shared common professional ground, similar concerns about academia, and an interest in curriculum and instruction. The experiences turned out to be successful due in part to our collective and individual efforts. By the end of my first year, the chair retired, and before I could even choose the first breaker or boulder on which to continue building upon my foundation, the dean of the college also left. Although this signaled an impending shift, I was unfazed.

The changing of the guard was to commence. The college got a new dean and I got a new chairperson, both of whom were internal candidates. I thought their familiarity would be beneficial. The department chairperson was a female, and the dean a male. I planned to stay the course and seek guidance along the way. I rationalized that no matter who assumed particular roles or positions, I would dig in my heels and remain stalwart at the helm of my work. I met my mentor to see if I was on track for receiving tenure and promotion. I reviewed guidelines and looked for research opportunities at every turn. I constructed a complex yet innovative scholarship agenda as I cross-pollinated with other departments by presenting with members within different departments; I was doing "bridgework." I also utilized my professional organizations statewide and on national levels and served in regional leadership capacities. I felt confident that I could make the case for tenure and promotion. I actually had the written support from the dean with regard to the productivity of the current year in my annual review letter, all of which was considered positive communication—I was on the right track.

The Challenge and the Process

I sought confirmation from tenured faculty in my department and was advised to go up for tenure a year early. I also had two other colleagues in allied departments in the college who did the same, and we worked together and gathered feedback on our work up to that point. As time progressed, I found that my process and my record would be challenged and questioned on multiple levels. From my perception, it seemed that advice and guidance on what was acceptable for my dossier changed based on the leadership more so than what was in the faculty handbook. It appeared as if the faculty handbook was being interpreted in several different ways, depending on whom you asked.

I knew that going up for tenure early was bold, but I wanted to scope out the lay of the shore to see what I was up against. It was not uncommon for faculty to go up a year early within my department, and I was not discouraged, so I forged ahead with my plan. Nevertheless, what I eventually found out was that it would be a false start. I compiled my dossier based on feedback from my pretenure (third-year review) submission and submitted it with a tentative confidence because I knew I had the basics of a good dossier, but I was curious of the perception of others. I chose to go up early because I wanted as much feedback as possible that could be used, if necessary, for the next academic year to make any needed adjustments to my body of work and productivity. My dossier made its way past my chairperson and department committees with approval. Though denied at the college level, I decided not to withdraw my submission and to have it continue on to be reviewed at the dean's level. My mentor also recommended this decision. I awaited feedback that would be constructive and help me assess what else would need to be added to my dossier the following year.

In the midst of my denial, I was told that someone heard the associate dean publicly discussing the color of the actual binder as well as the paper chosen to display my materials. I was taken aback as there were no requirements provided in the faculty handbook pertaining to color and/or appearance—only to how it should be organized and in what order. While the depth and breadth of the work were not discussed in her public statements, I wondered if the contents of my dossier had even been seen. I also wondered if my body of work was going to be judged by the dean without it being surveyed in its entirety.

I felt that the breach was an ethical issue of the grandest sort, but this was where my allies of multiple nationalities staged a coup. My White allies told me of the public and inappropriate discussions. My Black allies went back to the tenure and promotion guidelines to circumvent what was done. My East Indian allies prepared me for an optional approach and strategy. This was not a part of the lighthouse building I expected; this was not a part of my vision at all.

I planned a meeting with the dean and took my mentor with me for both support and reinforcement. The meeting took place over the holiday break, which was highly unusual. When we entered the meeting, the dean, who had previously been supportive of my agenda via public and private funding for my research projects, provided us an opinion of the issue. Suggestions about how to handle the issues, none of which included the gossip brought to my attention, were also discussed. Instead, I received a prescription of more publications and a suggestion that I reframe my narrative, all of which, I felt, was a simple fix, as did my mentor. I rallied my allies, and together we made the decision that I would remove my dossier from the process of tenure and promotion that year and gear up for the next year.

Restart Engaged

The restart of my promotion and tenure process left me more determined than ever. I had to dig into my resolve. I was anxious but confident that I could let my light shine and refocus the positive attention my dossier deserved. My allies and I planned to submit my dossier the following year. Consequently, another group of women of color were submitting their dossier as well, and we felt that there was power in numbers.

The calm before the storm appeared as many things. For me, I had time to retool and prepare for the upcoming year. It provided me with a time to address the gaps and to enjoy success in increments. This was a time to turn up the lights and to really shine like the beacon I had always envisioned.

The light began to shine, as my mentor and I were able to add additional information as encouraged by the dean and an additional year of teaching, service, and scholarship information. I was also able to include the award of external grants and reworked the narratives and sought additional feedback from faculty who had gone through the process successfully. I attended all of the tenure and promotion information meetings and read every "clarification of the process" e-mail from the associate deans. The process was billed as mystic, but I was still unfazed and determined. I researched every member of the department and college committees. I also researched how long ago they were awarded tenure and promotion. Moreover, I created vote scenarios or vote mockups, if you will, of faculty from whose votes I could secure with explicit knowledge and understanding of my work. I had plans to shine, but the restart would be a little more difficult than anticipated—a dark cloud was on its way.

STORMS AND SABOTAGE

Breakers in the Water

By the time the next year came around, the guard changed again. The dean left, and this time, the replacement was also an internal hire, who was also rumored to have made negative comments about my dossier. I believed that she was a sentinel who had no tolerance for the likes of my research agenda, my cross-departmental relationships, or me.

The first step of my resubmission process began with my department chair, and upon review, I was issued a letter of confidence and a signature to move my dossier to the next level. One hurdle crossed. The next steps had a positive outcome as well. I received a very positive letter of support from my department and this time from the college committee—another hurdle successfully crossed and I took each success and letter of support in stride. I savored each small victory and began to feel that my plan was close to coming to fruition. I was prepared to send my dossier up to the new dean. The letter of support from the college committee was extremely powerful. As I interpreted, all three letters supported me, affirmed my work, and identified my research agenda.

However, the breakers surfaced above the waterline and began to show themselves. It had long been a tradition that if a dossier makes it through all those levels and gets to the dean, the dean typically did not deviate from the decision of the college committee and the previous levels. However, this was so not the case. Instead the dean craftily dimmed the light that was designed to be a beacon. At the end of her review, I received a letter stating that I would not be supported for tenure and promotion.

In my opinion, the letter written by the dean represented sabotage and misinterpretation. The previous dean was available to give me feedback and recommendations when requested. He did not hesitate to share examples of similar issues from his own experiences when appropriate. But this was not the case with the current dean.

I had to still myself. I had to gather my thoughts, and I had to position myself into a defensive mode. I knew I had to fight, but I had to decide how far I was going to take the fight. I also had to decide if I would have support beyond the level of the dean, as historically, it was rare for a vice president or provost to overturn the decision of a dean. Once the dossier went up to the provost, I would not be able to restart my tenure and promotion process, and this represented my only opportunity to push for what I have earned.

Bringing in Reinforcements

As I knew this would not be easy, I began the rebuttal process, and I solicited the help of not only my allies but of an attorney. I had the support of allies; I had the recommendations of the college committee; but, most of all, I had me and I felt that all of this was enough. So I fought to stand and remain upright during the storm with the help of those who buoyed me up. We dissected the letter of nonsupport line by line, paralleling it with the documents that I had in my dossier refuting every claim bit by bit, character by character, punctuation by punctuation.

I did a number of things in terms of my rebuttal, including further clarifying my agenda in terms of my research by creating graphic organizers as a way to demonstrate and illustrate the intersection of my research. It was clear to everyone else, but for an administrator who appeared to wear the blinders of bias, it was as clear as mud. I was her intended target: even other members of the dominant group saw this and questioned the obvious injustice.

For example, my *service* at the institution was well received. However, a "college norm" was used to raise concerns about my *teaching*. The only issue was that these "norms" were never discussed previously. I was transparent in my reporting of teaching and was not aware of a College of Educator Preparation Program norm average that existed for evaluation purposes. After reading the concerns, I referred back to the faculty handbook, university policies, and the governing body's policies and found no such average or policies directed at comparing averages. In addition, information was not provided in the review letter as to an evaluation of norms across colleges. I thought it was relevant to note that during this time, I was faculty in more than one department and questioned in my rebuttal whether or not that was being considered.

I also had additional concerns due to comments in the area of *professional growth and development*. She provided commendation for my regional and national conferences, acknowledged my service on editorial boards for my discipline, and recognized my publications and presentations; a concern about the quality of some of my publications was somewhat disconcerting. Also, there were very strong accusations that I took very seriously. The response of my labor lawyer was to examine a possible EEOC case against the dean since she exhibited behavior that he deemed "aggressive" toward my body of work in the previous year. This was a very complex decision because I had chosen to go up for promotion with a class of faculty members who included women of color. The other two women of color were not having as much difficulty as I with the tenure and promotion process. One of my Black colleagues actually had a denial at a department level but was able to successfully rebut and move forward in the process.

In another turn of events, I reached out to the previous dean to receive feedback and suggestions about what I should do. It was his opinion that the interim dean was a "force to be reckoned with" and believed that the problems with me were more personal than professional, but he did not understand why—and neither could I. He also reiterated to me that it is very rare for a provost to overturn the decision of a dean. So I knew justice was not on my side of the shore.

It was very difficult to stand in the face of a storm realizing that this storm could be the last one I would ever weather on this shore; I could end up being on the losing end. The nonsupport of my dossier at the dean's level could have cost me my position at the institution and possibly my career in higher education. This type of storm could block the light of women of color and leave them on a shore, wandering in the dark searching for the light of academic and self-worth.

What to Do When Plan B Is Not Enough

The aforementioned situations led me, an academic, to wonder about what to do next. I had never considered giving up, and I had never considered leaving this institution without what I came to secure: tenure and promotion. I battled, struggled, and hid behind a smile, looking stalwart and upright, but on the inside, feeling defeated, angry, bitter, and disappointed by it all.

I had to make the decision as to whether I still wanted to try to shine on an unfriendly unwelcoming rocky shore or not. The decision was very difficult to make, so I sought advice on higher education blogs and read articles written by others who had been in the same situation as I. One article I read talked about the backlash of staying at an institution where you were not wanted, especially if litigation was involved and how people can make your life very uncomfortable when you were not wanted and your agenda was not of use.

However, I never even considered not fighting. I never considered going elsewhere. No one was going to kick me off my shore and out of the place that I had chosen to build my lighthouse. Nevertheless, the question loomed in my mind: did I still want to shine here? I reconsidered my gifts, skills, talents, and my ability to illuminate in the midst of a very hostile place. Would I look like I had given up if I had decided that my ability to shine *here* was unnecessary? Would I still be an effective advocate knowing that there would always be a shadow that loomed or someone who watched me as if a target was placed on my back? Would I be able to still do my most authentic social justice work and fight for my own rights as an academic and as a human being at the same time? What toll would this take on me, and would I still have any allies left? Would I be celebrated or ostracized if I chose to stay in an unwelcoming place with unwelcoming inhabitants only to lean on a small number of allies? Would I be ok if I were the only lighthouse on the shore? I questioned whether a battered, unwelcomed faculty member wearing a scarlet letter could effectively operate in parameters. Questions like would anyone within my department or college want to conduct research with me even popped into my mind. Would I still be selected with confidence to be a representative of the program at meetings and conferences? I had way more questions than answers and no home for my resolve.

How would I choose another shore on which to shine? If I chose to leave, how would I choose an appropriate place for me to shine, for my work to be illuminated, to uplift a community, to include faculty and students, and to add to the mission of that institution? I had to rethink the most appropriate place for my acts of service. There were a number of issues I had to consider in terms of location and occupying space. Was I willing to relocate my family, change my son's school, and sell my house—all for the sake of a place in higher education? Would I be willing to completely uproot my life, as I knew it, my village, my community, for the sake of being tethered to another shore that could end up being just as unfriendly and uncompromising?

An even greater question I asked myself was, was my light still significant? I began to question myself—if I could not advocate for me, how could I advocate for students, faculty, and other community members who need my voice? If I could not prove myself effective in my own cause, how could I take up the causes of others? And the questions kept coming.

I needed to rebuild. After months of going back and forth and months of rebuttals, consulting advisors, crying, and praying, I made the decision to build my lighthouse on another shore. I made the decision to take my career elsewhere, to a place more fertile, more challenging, and more uplifting. I wrestled with whether or not I was giving up, and I wrestled with an air of defeat. I understood that I was going to have to reconstruct and redefine myself so that I will be relevant on my next journey, my next assignment, and my next shore.

To start over, I had to be deliberate and calculated. It started with me believing in myself and not allowing others to dismantle or to chip away at my existence. It would begin with my confidence remaining intact despite an eroding situation. It would begin with an internal voice saying that I was not defined by my circumstances, only my response to them. I made the decision to apply for a new position knowing that others may look at the timing on my vita and see the time spent on an unforgiving and brutal shore. I had to decide how I would frame my experience as I spoke publicly, honestly, and yet with discretion. I had to interview as if this was a purposeful choice, and in many ways, it was.

I had to rebuild so that I would last. When given an opportunity to continue my career at another institution, I did not take my chance for granted and that approach worked in my favor. Nevertheless, in all the relief, vindication, and excitement, I had to remember my previous experience and reflect on the lessons learned. This called for the common sense and mother wit of generations of women in my family who survived similar situations. I knew that my light was still relevant and my light was worth its shine and I wanted to build myself, my career, and my existence in a manner that would support others who were trying to do the same thing. However, in order to be effective, I had to remember some very important lessons and these lessons led to my success in my new position.

Become Bigger, Brighter, Better: Lessons of Social Justice for the Righteously Indignant

It was not by coincidence that my professional and personal experiences mirrored my research agenda and the lessons of social justice. The lessons I taught so many other preservice teachers came back to teach me. If I wanted my light to shine brighter and if I wanted to rebuild bigger and better than before, there were a few things that I needed to remember:

1. Do not apologize for who you are and what you believe.
2. Joy is internal and is not equated with happiness, which is external, a lesson that was taught to me by my other mothers. Patricia Hill Collins (1991) defines the term *other mothers* as women who essentially nurture and function as mothers in the cultural parameters of fictive kinship and a cultural community. These other mothers for me included extended family, women in higher education and academia who were women of color, and White women who saw my value and worth because they had come before me and knew what I was up against.
3. You cannot run away from your destiny or who you were called to be, even if it is difficult, complicated, and understood by only a few who have also walked in my shoes. Fortunately, for me, during my academic career and educational life, I was surrounded by people in my educational life who experienced the same thing.
4. You will not always be rewarded for speaking your truth, whether it is convenient for someone or inconvenient for someone.
5. You are only an advocate when something is lost. There will be many people who claim to be allies and advocates, yet if they do not lose a piece of themselves in the fight, you have to be prepared to lose a piece of yourself.
6. It is alright to be righteously indignant. There is a problem with your soul if you see something wrong and you have no visceral response to the injustice.
7. You can be embattled and reborn, but you can still serve someone else in the midst of your own brokenness and despair.
8. Never say everything you are thinking but think about everything you say.
9. Despite the challenges, you have to continue to build regardless of the condition of the shore and know that sometimes your assignment in life will not be permanent. You are stationed at a particular shore for a particular time to complete a particular task. One minute beyond that time, you will miss your destiny.
10. No matter how painful, document your journey. There will be others coming along behind you who will need a roadmap to understand that their challenges are not unique and they will need to know that someone can survive whatever it is they are going through personally, academically, professionally, and spiritually.

My lighthouse was relevant, and it needed to continue to shine brightly. I did not and will not dim my light to make others more comfortable and me less effective at my overall mission and calling. Most important, there is life after enduring such a devastating loss. Resilience is key, and my light still shines, but it now lights a different shore.

REFERENCES

Constantine, M. G., & Sue, D. W. (2007, April 1). Perceptions of racial microaggressions among black supervisees in cross-racial dyads. *Journal of Counseling Psychology, 54*(2), 142–153.

Hill Collins, P. (1991). *Black feminist thought: Knowledge, consciousness and the politics of empowerment.* New York, NY: Routledge & Kegan Paul.

Thomas, U. (2015). *Lighthouse on the shore* (original poem). Atlanta, GA: Self-published.

U.S. Government Printing Office. (1916). *The United States lighthouse service, 1915.* Washington, DC: Author.

Chapter 8

The Golden Child

Jacqueline Johnson

In psychology, a golden child is the child chosen by the narcissistic parent to represent the parent's perceived wonderfulness. The regular rules don't apply to the child, and he or she gets the best of everything. The golden child serves as a medium through which the mother affirms who she believes herself to be. Similarly, *interest convergence*, a theory popularized by Derrick Bell (1980), suggests White elites advocate for the advancement of African Americans and other people of color only when such actions are deemed as also promoting or serving their own self-interests. The White elites, similar to the narcissistic mother, view the promotion of the African American or other people of color as merely a promotion of themselves. The person of color becomes the golden child to afford some benefit to the individual or individuals operating from a place of privilege and power. Dissimilar tokenism, which is often the result of compliance to some perceived or real regulation, the golden child, who is a person of color, is not advanced, so quotas can be met or sanctions can be thwarted. The golden child is selected in order for the narcissist or groups of narcissists to feel good about the good nature being showered on another. The golden child serves as proof that the narcissistic entity is as liberal and evolved as it believes itself to be.

There are two primary reasons that I chose the title, "The Golden Child," for this chapter. First, as mentioned previously, the field of psychology describes a golden child as one who receives a great deal of unmerited favor by a parent with a narcissistic personality disorder. The treatment of the child is not based upon the child possessing exceptional attributes above and beyond those of his or her siblings, but rather interactions are determined by the needs and predicaments of the narcissistic parent. The explanation for the treatment of the golden child by the narcissistic parent parallels the rationale for the favoritism I experienced as compared to other faculty members of color and, in some cases, Caucasian faculty members, in my opinion. I believe this to be especially evident given my obvious lack of appropriate credentials when I was first hired. The differential treatment I received after being hired further supports my theory and in turn justifies the title.

The second reason I chose the title is due to my personal connection to the field of counseling psychology. I earned an educational specialist (Ed.S.) degree in counseling and human rehabilitative services, and I have studied the works of Jung, a Swiss psychiatrist and psychotherapist. Given my own background, choosing a title for a chapter about me that in a small way relates to who I am as an individual seemed very appropriate.

In my chapter, I deem all the faculty and administrators who played a role in hiring and promoting me to serve their own needs and predicaments as the narcissistic parent/mother. My discussion is not based on one particular woman. Both male and female faculty members showed favoritism toward me above that shown to my other colleagues of color, largely Black. It is one's motivation (both conscious and unconscious) that makes him or her the narcissistic parent, not one's gender.

As institutions of higher education have embraced the notion that it is in their own self-interest to diversify the members of the academy and demonstrate a valuing of diversity, more and more opportunities have opened up for faculty of color to live the life of a golden child. Typically, faculty of color face many challenges in academe such as the "undervaluation of their research interest," "challenges to their credentials and intellect," unrealistic expectations in regard to their being the authority on issues related to their racial or ethnic group, and accent discrimination (Turner, González, & Wood, 2008, p. 143). Yet, few select individuals, who are bequeathed with the honor of being chosen as the minority "golden child," are given privileges and opportunities that other faculty of color are not offered or are even aware exist. This chapter presents the story of one such faculty member and the sometimes shocking, preferential treatment received during her tenure at a midsized university in the Southeast.

MY BACKGROUND

I am an African American female born in 1968. I was born just 14 days before the assignation of Dr. Martin Luther King. Thankfully, I was born in Minneapolis, Minnesota, and that city was far removed from the racism of the South. My mother's best friend, Rita, was a White woman, and Rita's boyfriend was an African American. My parents went on dates with Rita and her boyfriend all of the time. I had a White babysitter who kept me while my mother worked at Sears and my father attended the University of Minnesota.

My brother's best friends were White, and he rode the bus to school every weekday with his White friends. This kind of situation is rare even in modern times.

I was born into a life that was filled with positive experiences with persons of other races, and with only a few exceptions my whole life has been this way. When my family moved back to South Florida, where both of my parents grew up, I did not experience racism for we moved into an all-Black area of Belle Glade, Florida, and I don't remember ever meeting a White person in that town. My family moved into my biological grandfather's home. He was a prominent physician in the community, and everyone knew our family's name. In fact, my biological grandfather had a library named after him in Fort Lauderdale, Florida, where my parents grew up. After moving out of my grandfather's house, my family moved into a working-class neighborhood where the family next door to us was comprised of a Puerto Rican father, a White mother, and two biracial daughters. The other families in the neighborhood were White. I don't recall any African American neighbors. If we had any, they were very few. Again, my brother's friends were all White, and we attended a predominantly White elementary school. I don't recall experiencing any racism other than offensive comments from our White male neighbor who rode a motorcycle and looked a lot like a young Clint Eastwood. He endearingly called me a "cute little monkey." I was an excellent tree climber when I was young, and he allowed my brother, his friends, and I to climb the tree in his front yard. Sometimes, when he would arrive home from work, he would walk past the tree and say something like, "Hello, cute little monkey." I actually don't think he thought he was being offensive. In fact, I didn't even feel offended until as an adult I reflected on the memories I had of those days.

It was not until my family moved to a home in Lake Worth, Florida, when I began to have repeated experiences with discrimination. I use the word *discrimination* for while I had a few encounters with those I presumed to be racists, overall the kind of discrimination I experienced was classism. The school I attended was a predominantly White school, and the White students lived in a more affluent side of town. Often, the most affluent students looked down upon anybody, White or Black, who was not as affluent as they were. I remember once my brother invited one of his classmates over to our home and he commented to my brother we lived in a shack. My family remained in Lake Worth throughout my junior high and high school education. Interestingly, with a few exceptions, my experiences with racism were the result of encounters with prejudice White, female teachers. Much like the hateful characters portrayed in movies such as *Rosewood*, *12 Years a Slave*, and *Underground*, they treated me with disrespect and felt the need to put me in my place. Yet the majority of my experiences with Whites were positive. Most of my closest friends were White, and one of my closest school friends was one of the more popular White baseball players at my school. We sat next to each other in class and walked home as far as our paths aligned on multiple occasions. I cared for him and he cared for me. I was so well accepted by White males that my boyfriend from 8th through 11th grades was White and was a close friend of my brother. Our families were so close, his mother taught me how to drive, and I ate dinner at his house as much as my parents would allow. Even after our relationship ended, I dated a few other White males before leaving for college.

Truthfully, it was not until I attended Florida State University (FSU) when I really developed my Afrocentric identity. I finally ran into other African Americans who were just like me. I also discovered the beautiful mecca of African American males that attended Florida Agricultural and Mechanical University. Once I realized I was not the odd African American female who was more White-like than Black, but rather a member of a unique group of smart, intelligent brothers and sisters, I was a changed woman. I didn't even want a part of that old life. My only experience with racism at FSU was again at the hands of a White female teacher. My internship teacher was so prejudiced that my university supervisor removed me from her classroom. I was moved to a better placement with a very welcoming White female teacher and was very successful. I did so well in my new placement that the school hired me once I completed my program. I did not have a lot of White friends during my undergraduate years, but on more than one occasion I did go on a date with a White male. My experiences in graduate school were much like the kinds of experiences I have had my whole life. Overwhelmingly, I had positive relationships with other races and have no memories of blatant racism. Even after graduating with my bachelor's degree and working as a teacher, I had positive work experiences with persons of other races. The director of the second school at which I accepted a position was such a good friend to me that I considered him a second father. He gave me a car to drive and let me live in his second home while in graduate school. He even helped me move to Georgia in 1996. He would talk to me about life, including my boyfriends, and even edited my graduate school papers for me. Without him, I may not be where I am today for I learned so much from him.

I have no doubt my having a long history of positive experiences with other races, particularly Caucasians, has shaped my beliefs and values. I believe in the good of all races and have repeatedly benefited from the goodness of Whites. It is not a surprise that I would be favored as a college professor for being cared for and treated with positive regard by those of other races is theme that has manifested itself throughout my life. I was literally born to be a golden child, and that is exactly what my experience has been in academia.

THE BEGINNING

From the beginning, my path was one of favor and one in which the typical rules of engagement did not apply. In 1998, I was a 30-year-old, African American woman, nearing the end of my doctoral program from a research one institution in the South. Since I had finished all of my coursework, I was now free to work a full-time job. So I began looking for positions in my field that matched my skills and experience. In surveying various job position announcements, I discovered that a university about 45 minutes from where I lived had an opening for the director of the Early Childhood Education Lab School. Having worked part time for the past four years as an assistant director at a local child care center, I thought the position was perfect. Not only would I be able to continue to acquire experience in my field, but once I earned my doctorate degree, I may have an inroad to a tenure-track position. Therefore, I decided to apply for the position. Shortly after I applied, I was given an on-campus interview.

The interview went very well, and I felt good about my chances at getting the job. Unbeknownst to me at that time, and much in line with practices in the South, there was a retired teacher who was connected to the university whom the search committee already had pegged for the position. Naturally, she was offered the position, and that should have been the end of my story with this particular institution. But it was not. Apparently, after meeting me, the committee had much bigger and better plans for me. The committee member, who called me to explain that I was not selected for the director position, followed that explanation with an invitation to apply for a full-time instructor position. I was told I would not have to interview again and basically the job was mine, if I wanted it. This invitation completely caught me by surprise—so much so that I asked the person to confirm what was said to me.

Acquiring a university position was my end goal anyway, and to be offered this position with no effort on my part was beyond my wildest expectations. Naturally, I went to campus and filled out the necessary paperwork and was hired shortly thereafter. That experience was the first of many golden child experiences I would have at this institution. I was afforded privileges that were not readily afforded to minorities and given opportunities for which I didn't even ask.

While the aforementioned story may not seem like an extraordinary beginning or one indicative of a golden child, I assure you that it was. Over the years, I learned that it was not unusual for a search committee to have an inside candidate. Yet it was rare to be turned down for the position for which one applied and in that same conversation to be asked to apply for an even more desirable position. In addition, the search committee selected me for a position above other applicants without my having earned a master's degree or doctorate degree in the specific field for which I was being hired. Looking back on it now, I would have never done that had I been on the search committee. In fact, I am a firm believer that in higher education, credentials and infield experience matter greatly. But, again, credentials did not matter when you were the golden child.

My new colleagues wanted a feather in their cap, and what a pretty feather I was. I was young, single, childless, and graduated from research one institutions for my bachelors, masters, and soon to be doctorate degree. They had essentially won the minority golden child lottery, and they knew it. No one cared that my degrees were in a different field—they wanted to diversify the faculty with a minority female, and the female they wanted was me. In the end, I was invited to apply for a position for which I knew nothing about and one that was most likely never advertised.

THE EARLY YEARS: NOTHING BUT THE BEST

My first year as a tenure-track faculty member was filled with excitement and a great deal of faculty support. At that time, I had no idea that this level of support was unusual. However, now that I am in my 17th year as a member of academia, there have only been a few faculty members I have witnessed receiving the level of support I received, and those that received the support were all Caucasian. The support I received spanned all aspects of tenure and promotion at this institution. Typically, literature related to the retention of African American faculty holds that faculty of color should have fellow African American colleagues as mentors (Thurman, 2002). Well, I had no mentors for I was the only African American female in the college. However, I did not need them. I had White mentors: both male and female. Some were middle aged, while others were older. They knew how to navigate their world, and they were determined to help me learn how to do so as well. They interacted with me as if I was one of their own and modeled exactly what needed to be done. In every area of my professional life, I had support. This support spanned teaching, service, and scholarship. Using Japanese terminology I entered a dojo (school) on being tenured and promoted, and my senseis (teachers) were plentiful.

In the area of teaching, I was paired with a popular teacher who was so well organized that she had lesson plans for every course session. Anne gave me everything. When I say everything, I mean everything. She gave me her books, her weekly class notes, her quizzes, her overhead slides, her in-class activities, and the materials needed for those activities. Now, in our digital age, all these are available via a course platform such as Chalk & Wire, CourseDen, or LiveText, and to share them, all one has to do is grant access to his or her course. But, back then, the lecture notes were handwritten and the books were either hardback or paperback. Basically, all I had to do was teach what she had prepared and grade the assignments. Because she was such a strong teacher, so was I. My first-year teaching reviews were very strong.

The next year, Anne left the university to support her husband with his growing business. Needless to say, everything she had in her office was mine for the taking. Remember, I knew this woman for a little over a year, and she had been on faculty at the institution for a number of years. Yet she left it all to me and no one else she had come to know. Her library was extensive and easily totaled over $500 or $600. I remember being thankful for having immediate access to a library that could rival any scholar in the field—for free. It was a scholar's dream, and I still use some of her resources for my courses and for research.

In the area of service, things were quite the same. In my first year, I was completely excused from any service in order to focus on writing. After having a year to focus on writing and presenting, I was then placed on several influential college committees. Although I was a junior faculty member and far from going up for tenure, I was put on committees whose membership was only senior, tenured faculty. My faculty advisor for my dissertation told me it was important to get on high-profile committees in so that my service would be highly regarded, and that is exactly what happened to me. I was placed on the Faculty Governance Committee, the most influential committee in the college. I was also nominated to serve on the Personnel Committee, the committee that dealt with the process for tenure and promotion and fielded faculty concerns regarding the operation of the college. This committee also organized elections. So there I was, the only brown face in the room, speaking up and making decisions about tenure and promotion while not even having completed a third-year review.

Being a typical junior faculty member, I spoke up often and shared my opinion because I didn't know any better. Yet, rather than being put in my place, I was all the more respected. My growth in stature and influence continued, and I was elected the chair of Faculty Governance. I then became a member of an influential university committee. This position, which was typically reserved for tenured faculty, benefited me in many ways. Having tenured faculty members know and respect me helped in developing a good reputation in the college. In addition, the dean attended meetings, which allowed me the opportunity to make myself known to him. I was then nominated and placed on university committees, and it was not long before I was made the chair of two of the university committees on which I served. By the time I went up for tenure, my institutional service was stellar.

In looking back at the favor I received in the area of scholarship, I still find much of it shocking and mind-boggling. In my second year as a faculty member, the dean of the college wrote a university-system grant, a grant that was awarded and handed over to me. Yes, while she did all the work, I was made a PI and was the manager of the entire project. I was even assigned a graduate assistant. The grant was over $100,000. As was the case with my being hired, I knew nothing about this grant. I did not ask to receive the grant, yet here it was, dropped right into my lap. The dean knew it was a controversial move, so much so that I was not to talk to others about the "arrangement". At that time, there were approximately 80 tenure-track faculty members within the college, most of whom would have loved to have had a grant dropped in their lap and who were probably more knowledgeable than I with regard to grants. Then there were others who, I am sure, needed the boost of a grant to help them earn tenure. To this day, I am still in awe of the level of support this dean gave to me. As she knew would be the case, throughout the tenure and promotion process, I was given credit for receiving external funding for a grant that I had absolutely nothing to do with; I did not even write the annual reports.

In regard to making presentations, it was more of the same. Senior faculty approached me and asked what I was doing with regard to presenting. I knew little to nothing about making scholarly presentations and had not submitted anything other than the one presentation I submitted on my dissertation research with the help of my faculty advisor. I was terrified at the thought. Nevertheless, I had no reason to be afraid of because my colleagues were more than willing to provide support.

For my first presentation, Leslie, my office neighbor, suggested I present at the conference where she presented the year before. She gave me her presentation from the previous year along with a copy of her conference proposal. She also helped vet topics for my proposal as well as helped me write the proposal. Of course, it was accepted, and, then, I was off to the races.

After the aforementioned experience, I went from being fearful to truly believing that getting a proposal accepted was easy, and, truthfully, it was. At this point, my role on Faculty Governance Council paid off. Most faculty members knew me and I knew them, so I was able to collaborate with faculty members from both inside and outside of my college. I presented with others at first, and then I began to present on my own. I quickly went from state and regional presentations to national and international presentations, with cost being my only limitation when it came to the number of international presentations completed. By the time I went up for tenure, I had made 22 presentations, averaging more than four presentations a year.

EXTRAORDINARY TENURED SUPPORT

When the time came for me to apply for tenure, I thought I was in good shape, but I did not want to be overly confident. For that reason, I began seeking the opinions of knowledgeable faculty. I went to my former department chair, who provided me with a wealth of knowledge. In addition, he recommended faculty members of whom I should ask for added feedback. Again, the support came from everywhere. Not only did I have colleagues within my department review my material, but I also received reviews from faculty members from other departments. In fact, even the associate dean of the college looked over my material and gave me feedback. I felt as though they all had a vested interest in my success and wanted me to be successful in my application for both tenure and promotion. With the excellent feedback and special treatment I had received over my first five years, I was ready. As a result, I received unanimous support at every level. The mission was accomplished, and the prophecy was fulfilled.

POSTTENURE AND BEYOND

I continuously received incredible support and respect after being granted tenure and promotion to associate professor. A faculty member in another department recommended me to a consulting firm, so I was able to begin working as an educational consultant and eventually owned my own consulting business. I never paid a dime to advertise and grossed as much as $30,000 in one year. I also collaborated with a colleague, and using an idea we learned at training, we developed a teacher resource that yielded five books. One year, we were even the featured authors at the most prestigious annual conference in our field and were given the opportunity to host a book signing. The books brought notoriety to my name in our local area, which afforded me the opportunity to serve on multiple grants that partnered with local school systems.

The continued support and favor also made getting promoted to full professor easy. I was promoted to full professor at the age of 43, and in the field that I am in, many begin their careers in higher education at this age. But for me, I had done it all. So much had been literally handed to me, so it only made sense for me to take the next step. So I put my materials together, and again, I was unanimously supported throughout the process.

Since being promoted, my circle of influence has expanded. Shortly after being promoted, I was nominated and selected to serve on the most influential committee a university could form, the search committee for the president of the university. There were only 18 members on this committee, including prominent community members, representatives from every division in the university, and the alumni association president. In a university with over 400 faculty and staff, one can only imagine how desperate some were to be chosen to be on the search committee. There were only two minorities on the committee, one male and one female. I was that female. It was an incredible honor! But one would expect nothing less from the golden child. Alas, the legend of the golden child continued.

Currently, I am a department chair. I am one of only three African American chairs within the entire university, both of whom have been employed at the university longer than I. In fact, one has been at the university since the early 1980s. But, who knows, perhaps, once a decade, a chosen one appears and in the 1980s, the chosen one was him. In the new millennium, that chosen one was me. I never interviewed for the position, nor did I fill out an application. As was done previously, I was selected for the position, and even though I have been in my new position only for two months, I have already engaged in conversations about my being promoted to associate dean within the next year or so. I have little doubt it will happen. It will be just one more experience in line with all the others.

In every way, my experience as a woman of color in academia defied the norm. Rather than being marginalized and isolated as described in the literature (Caldwell & Stewart, 2001; Collins, 1986; Garrison-wade, Diggs, Estrada, & Galindo, 2012), I was valued, respected, and embraced. Rather than receiving less mentoring than my White counterparts (Ashburn, 2007), I received more, from faculty of all ranks and positions. Rather than having to fight for tenure and promotion, I was supported before, during, and after the processes. I have and continue to live what can easily be seen as a charmed life in academia. Unfortunately, I cannot say I owe it all to my own talent and ability for I have seen more talented colleagues treated unfairly. I have seen my intellectual superiors casted out with reckless abandonment. I have witnessed racial and ethnic discrimination over and over again. But nothing of the sort has ever even come near me. I was and still am a golden child. I am Exhibit A, showing the entire world that racism is not a problem at our institution. I am living proof that my university embraces women and minorities and is full of individuals willing to help them succeed. Unfortunately, the opposite is actually true. Both women and people of color are continuously marginalized and treated unfairly at my institution. In the past year, there were three faculty members who considered suing the institution. All of which had fairly strong cases. The reality of the inequitable treatment my colleagues received compared to me may have stirred up negative emotions. But I cannot personally speak to that matter for if my colleagues were angry or jealous, I was not privy to that information. In fact, I felt supported by my colleagues of color. If I had "haters," I was oblivious to them. I sincerely sympathized with the discrimination my colleagues experienced, and I think they all knew it. I fully subscribe to the words of Dr. Martin Luther King that "injustice anywhere is a threat to justice everywhere." Despite being a privileged faculty member, I have done all that I knew to do to work toward my colleagues receiving the justice they each deserve. I have helped write tenure and promotion rebuttal letters, and I have spoken with university administration on behalf of others. I have spoken up open forums about the prejudice I have witnessed, and I have had open conversations with colleagues who have been discriminated against and promised I would go to court with them should they decide to take such actions. I have not feared losing my status as a golden child because I know the institution needs me. I know that if I go down for standing up for others who have been discriminated against, the whole facade is over. There is nothing left to point to counter the claims of racial discrimination. The narcissist mother would have to face her shortcomings, and she would never let that happen. I feel secure not only because I have been in the right, but I know it would be too costly to take me down. Every case of discrimination would be more credible and even more winnable. I am confident I could readily win a court case for the retaliation experienced and possibly even retire on the settlement. Yet I try as I might to work against injustice. I have had little success in preventing my colleagues of color from experiencing discrimination. Those in positions of power and influence treat them and me as they wish. Like Bell (1980) asserts, it all depends on what has been deemed in their best interest. To them, we are both little more than pieces on their chessboard to be strategically disposed of or manipulated as deemed necessary.

The persistent underrepresentation of faculty of color in higher education continues to serve as proof that institutions of higher education continue to discriminate against faculty of color in their hiring and retention practices. Faculty members of color are not fooled by the presence of a golden child. Much like the sibling(s) of a golden child in a family, they know who the favored child is and they realize that the golden child's experiences will not be the same as their own. While the golden child can do no wrong, for many faculty of color, they can do no right. I. Furthermore, they recognize that the existence of a golden child can actually work against them with regard to unfair and biased treatment. The golden child gives the institution a counterexample to put forth when claims of discrimination are launched against it. In fact, these select individuals give counterexamples to the media and lawmakers to rebuke the claims that racism is at an all-time high. These counterexamples do not exist by chance. Just like I was, they are strategically selected and promoted. Perhaps, the value in my story is not merely to tell the life of a golden child but to reveal the damage that can and does occur when institutions utilize these exceptions to remain superficially diverse versus seeking opportunities to become meaningfully inclusive.

REFERENCES

Ashburn, E. (2007). Survey identifies colleges that know how to keep junior faculty members happy. *Chronicle of Higher Education, 53*(22), 22–28.

Bell, D. (1980). *Brown v. board of education* and the interest-convergence dilemma. *Harvard Law Review, 93*(3), 518–523.

Caldwell, L. D., & Stewart, J. B. (2001). Rethinking W. E. B. Dubois "double consciousness": Implications for retention and self-preservation in the academy. In L. Jones (Ed.), *Retaining African Americans in higher education: Challenging paradigms for retaining students, faculty & administrators* (pp. 193–205). Sterling, VA: Stylus Publishing.

Collins, P. H. (1986). Learning from the outsider within: The sociological significance of black feminist thought. *Social Problems, 33*(6), 14–32.

Garrison-Wade, D., Diggs, G. A., Estrada, D., & Galindo, R. (2012). Lift every voice and sing: Faculty of color face the challenges of the tenure track. *Urban Review, 44*(1), 90–112. doi: http://dx.doi.org/10.1007/s11256-011-0182-1

Thurman, T. (2002). Are we there yet? Retaining faculty of color. *Black Issues in Higher Education, 19*(13), 36.

Turner, C. S. V., González, J. C., & Wood, J. L. (2011). Faculty of color in academe: What 20 years of literature tell us. In S. R. Harper & J. F. L. Jackson (Eds.), *Introduction to American higher education* (pp. 41–73). New York, NY: Routledge.

Chapter 9

Thematic Analysis

Karen Harris Brown and
Patricia Alvarez McHatton

This book seeks to inform, empower, and provide a voice to faculty of color at predominately White institutions (PWIs). It offers a vivid account of the lived experiences of select faculty of color at these institutions. The narratives are from faculty who identify themselves as *being of color* and include Black, Asian, and Latin@. Further, the narratives also provide gendered perspectives as both females and males contributed to the book. In addition to gaining a sense of the lived experiences of contributing faculty, we sought to identify to what extent these experiences contained similar themes, which could be used to develop systems of support to improve recruitment and retention of faculty of color in PWIs. The following research questions guided the development of this book:

1. What are the experiences of faculty of color at PWIs of higher education?
2. In what ways do faculty of color at PWIs of higher education cope with or handle struggles or defeats and successes in the workplace?
3. In what ways can college or university administrators and colleagues support and retain faculty of color?

The editors used the following verification procedures to ensure reliability and validity when establishing themes: member checks; interrater reliability through consensus; description of researcher bias; and rich, thick description (Creswell, 1998; Creswell & Miller, 2000). Member checks were conducted throughout the process. Authors received multiple opportunities to clarify and revise their narratives and also reviewed the findings to ensure they have accurately captured the underlying themes of their experiences. Each chapter was read by at least two of the editors who individually analyzed and coded the narratives read. All editors convened to review codes. Rather than seek a particular percent of agreement, editors discussed discrepancies and reached consensus on final coding. Codes were then collapsed into six themes based on common characteristics.

CONTEXT

Context refers to historical factors as well as individuals' experiences within their institutions that play a role in how they are perceived by others. For example, An shares how her experiences in Korea sheltered her from the reality of living in a dictatorship. It was not until she came to the United States when she became aware of the role of the United States in world politics, anticommunist nationalism, pro-Americanism, and anti-Japanese and anti-Chinese sentiments within the United States. This experience led to a loss of innocence, something that was shared by several of the other authors. Johnson relayed occurrences that reflected both positive and disturbing experiences as she lived within racially heterogeneous and homogeneous settings. Glenn begins his narrative juxtaposing his experiences with his son's eligibility for the gifted and talented program coming into question and his own coming of age as a Black male encumbered with the responsibility of ameliorating others' discomfort of his being. He provides a comprehensive overview of the cost of being a Black make—loss of opportunity, loss of life—as well as the need to attend to matters of dress, speech, grooming, and conduct. This dual consciousness is also expressed by Smith who shares similar experiences regarding the need to represent in particular, acceptable ways. Ramanathan presents a more global identity, noting that her position as an Indian American has provided her with a vast amount of academic and social capital that nonetheless came into question as she sought promotion to full professor.

Contributing authors worked in PWIs and in education; therefore, not only were they in the minority as faculty, they also taught predominately White, female, middle-class students who likely had rarely (if ever) experienced being taught by someone of color. This led to concerns by Smith regarding the experiences of the few students of color in his classroom as he fostered a safe place for *all* students to speak openly and "just say it."

TENURE

The theme of tenure includes the pretenure, tenure, posttenure, and promotion processes. All of the authors referenced this theme in their narratives. Glenn, Smith, and Guerra are all pretenure. An received tenure and promotion while writing her chapter. She uses the term *exhausting* to describe her experience with the process. Thomas was denied tenure. She discusses her experiences with not receiving support from some administrators, despite receiving support from her supervisor and colleagues in the process. Glenn, Smith, and Guerra described the tenure process as ambiguous and "cloaked in secrecy," and some expressed fear of the process—expressions shared by most faculty, including those who are not of color.

Both Johnson and Ramanathan are posttenure although their experiences in reaching this designation are drastically different. Johnson is a full professor, and Ramanathan is an associate professor who did not receive promotion to full professor. Johnson received a great deal of faculty support from White mentors who helped her navigate the academy in teaching, research, and service. She was provided a reduced service load in her first year in order to focus on her writing after which she was assigned to influential committees that provided high visibility within the institution. Her input was valued. She notes her experiences are not the norm, having been privy to the experiences of other faculty of color who were not welcomed to the extent she was.

Ramanathan's challenges took place when she first went up for promotion. Prior to this, she did not experience any challenges with achieving tenure and promotion at two PWIs. She was threatened with being placed on a growth plan and was told she was not a good teacher and that her research was lacking. The threat was dismissed when she decided to pull her dossier from review. When she attempted to submit it the following year, the threat returned and she was subsequently denied promotion.

Concerns over student teaching evaluations especially when teaching courses that may result in student resistance are expressed by Smith who notes, "Fear of poor student evaluations can make you respond in ways contrary to your preparation and principles." Likewise, Guerra notes that some faculty preferred to "give in" rather than engage in power struggles with students. Each of these authors indicates a need to fit into the mainstream culture in order to be successful in his or her bid for tenure. For example, Ramanathan sought approval after her first year to assert her native identity by wearing her traditional Indian attire. She also expresses some challenge with the emphasis on peer-reviewed journal publications rather than policy-related reports, which are necessary and relevant in developing regions where her interests lie. While some of the authors indicate being overwhelmed with service and teaching, An indicates she had limited opportunities to engage in service. One author, Johnson, discusses her relative ease in moving through the pretenure, tenure, and posttenure processes and the support she received from others as she went through each phase of the process.

CONFLICT

The theme of conflict encompasses experiences with colleagues, administrators, students, and teaching. Conflict with colleagues often took the form of microaggressions—subtle, denigrating everyday exchanges between well-intentioned, but unaware members of the dominant culture and certain individuals as a result of their group membership (Orelus, 2013, Paludi, 2012; Sue, 2010). For example, Guerra indicates reticence speaking up in meetings or engaging in e-mail exchanges as a result of overhearing comments regarding her inability to speak or write English. Thomas discusses learning from colleagues that an administrator made inappropriate comments about her, rather than the quality of her work, in a public setting. Glenn describes how others respond to his questioning as a challenge.

Conflict with students most often pertained to teaching situations. An was accused of being radical, anti-American, communist, or crazy. Her accented English and inclusion of controversial topics in her social studies methods course led to low teacher evaluations. Like An, Guerra also experienced challenges in her teaching due to her accented English as well as her discussion of culturally responsive pedagogy within her math methods courses. Students refused to meet her to discuss the issues they were having, and when she addressed her concerns with her supervisor she was told to "apologize for her accent" and to try to become more like her students (i.e., White). Ramanathan was removed as the instructor of record for a class in the middle of the semester and without due process, following student complaints to her supervisor; she was not given the opportunity to see the complaints or provide a rebuttal. In her narrative, she further discusses her students' assumptions about her experience with the U.S. educational system when they see her with non-Western attire. While they have reportedly described her as having desirable personal attributes (e.g., qualified and proficient in English), she perceived this to be reflective of a lack of attention to her persona as an ethnic being and suggestive of a lack of comfort with discussions on race and ethnicity.

Glenn's students had limited interactions with those of other races, and most had never had experienced a Black teacher, especially a Black male. He discusses a White student's outward expression of fear taking a class in which he, a Black male, was the instructor of record, because of her negative experience with three Black males unrelated to this faculty member. Smith, who teaches courses on multicultural education, purposefully developed strategies to respond to student resistance. He recognizes the importance of providing students a safe space to "just say it" while acknowledging his own challenges in negotiating his response to their honest but troubling exclamations. His efforts to support students in their growth have challenges as "honest exclamations can be troubling and concerns over how students interpret responses and student evaluations exist."

IMPACT

The theme of impact applies to the effects on the authors as a result of their experiences. Guerra discusses feeling silenced, but acknowledging through self-reflection that she has in fact silenced herself as well. Both she and An discuss the alienation they feel from colleagues due to language or international barriers. The impact on Glenn has been that of cognitive load. He expresses feeling overburdened with teaching and service, similar to other tenure-track faculty including White males. An important distinction Glenn posits is that performance by a White male is generally viewed as reflective of the individual, while performance by a Black male is often generalized to the general population; thus, there is intense pressure to positively "represent." Ramanathan describes self-recognition of her own privilege when she began her doctoral studies. She was deemed qualified to teach multicultural and ESOL courses as a result of her "minority" status and experiences due to living in other countries. It appears she is determined qualified by virtue of her interests and identity, rather than her credentials.

SUPPORT

Discussions related to support focused on privilege and mentorship. Johnson describes the assistance of White mentors, who helped her navigate the academy in all three traditional areas related to tenure and promotion: teaching, service, and scholarship. Her experience has been one of favor and one in which typical rules of engagement did not apply. Her narrative provides readers with information about supports she received beyond that which was available to others. Reportedly, her experience in academe defied the norm. Guerra, while reporting very different experiences, discusses her perceived privilege as a university professor and the ability it affords her to make change. Ramanathan discusses the support she received from colleagues and family as she tried to navigate the posttenure promotion process. Thomas describes her support from a former administrator, an assigned mentor, and other faculty of color as she navigated the tenure and promotion process.

RESPONSE

Response pertains to how each author responded to the experiences that he or she had. In all cases, the authors reveal a process in which they reconceptualized their identity as ethnic beings. An changed her teaching style, decreased her talking time during class in order to assist with the challenges students claimed to have with her accent, and became transparent and vulnerable in order to make the classroom a safe place for her students. While these are good pedagogical strategies in general, she perceived them to be essential for her as an Asian teacher. In addition, her personal experiences fostered a desire to empower teacher candidates as antiracist, social justice–oriented citizens on a local and global level. Glenn discusses the need for reconciliation and negotiation within White spaces and describes defensive and offensive techniques or strategies to signal harmlessness while actively disabling stereotypes. He exists within a reality where as a Black male when vocal he is perceived as challenging and when silent he is perceived as angry. Smith was able to distance himself from his teaching evaluations and learned how, when, and why to code switch. Ramanathan and Thomas sought support from colleagues and family. Johnson and Ramanathan state a commitment to working to ensure colleagues receive the justice they deserve and being vocal at forums designed to address institutional racism and enhance institutional climate.

While quests for clarification are viewed as a challenge, Glenn refused to be silenced in this area, continuing to self-advocate. Glenn believes seeking clarification will benefit others as well as himself. Guerra came to the realization of her complicity in her silencing. With this acknowledgment comes a decision to intentionally speak up, not just for herself but for others as well. Additional examples of self-advocacy include setting a goal to break the imposition of self-silence, seeking support from colleagues and family, wearing traditional Indian attire without hesitancy, and using this non-Western attire to make a statement, both professionally and politically. As a result of Ramanathan's experiences and self-advocacy, a diversity committee was constituted and opportunities to identify discriminatory practices and action steps to promote equity were provided.

SUMMING IT UP

An important thread that spans all of the narratives is resiliency and perseverance. Each has experienced various forms of resistance and microaggressions. All express in some form their understanding of the need to represent in ways that defy stereotypes and demonstrate the contributions they can make to the institution and the profession. All offer suggestions for navigating academia as a faculty of color.

REFERENCES

Creswell, J. W. (1998). *Qualitative inquiry and research design: Choosing among five traditions* (p. 179). Thousand Oaks, CA: Sage.

Creswell, J. W., & Miller, D. L. (2000). Determining validity in qualitative inquiry. *Theory into Practice, 39*, 124–130.

Orelus, P. W. (2013). The institutional cost of being a professor of color: Unveiling micro-aggression, racial [in]visibility, and racial profiling through the lens of critical race theory. *Current Issues in Education, 16*(2), 1–11. Retrieved from http://cie.asu.edu/ojs/index.php/cieatasu/article/viewFile/1001/485

Paludi, M. A. (2012). *Managing diversity in today's workplace: Strategies for employees and employers.* Santa Barbara, CA: Praeger.

Sue, D. W. (2010). *Microaggressions in everyday life: Race, gender, and sexual orientation* (p. xvi). Hoboken, NJ: John Wiley & Sons.

Chapter 10

Faculty of Color Navigating Higher Education

Karen Harris Brown and
Patricia Alvarez McHatton

In this final chapter, we provide recommendations and call for actions based on the themes that emerged from the narratives. These recommendations serve to inform administrators and faculty of efforts that can potentially support faculty of color, made by faculty of color. The first set of recommendations pertains to the themes: *context*, *response*, and *impact*. Evident across chapters within this book and the literature is the scarcity of faculty of color at PWIs. One consequence of this reality is a lack of a critical mass of individuals cognizant of issues significant to members of this population who can bring these issues to the forefront. Another concern is a focus on race as the predominant factor when addressing issues related to faculty of color. Thus, it is essential to address diversity such that efforts attend to all faculty of color including subgroups (e.g., Asian faculty, Latin@ faculty). In addition, several of the authors indicated feeling isolated and silenced not only by White colleagues but also by colleagues from other underrepresented groups. Therefore, an important consideration is attending to both within and across group factors based on racial, ethnic, and international status.

Another theme that emerged from the narratives pertained to conflicts experienced with administrators, colleagues, and students. Often, these conflicts were characteristic of acts of microaggression. Authors discussed the resistance they faced due to the differences they represented in thought, language or English proficiency, accent, and so on. A greater appreciation for difference and awareness of the challenges that faculty of color face may be facilitated through professional learning experiences in culturally responsive interactions. These activities may reduce acts of microaggression, discrimination, and stereotyping and increase empathy. In colleges of education, there is a great deal of emphasis on preparing culturally responsive candidates. This is done through a variety of activities including readings, field experiences in diverse settings, and cross-cultural activities requiring candidates to participate in settings that position them as the "other." Institutions regularly require completion of training modules related to a variety of topics including sexual harassment, research, and utilizing university vehicles, to name a few. Perhaps, a more substance approach, similar to that which candidates take part in, should be undertaken to foster an environment that is culturally responsive and supportive.

The final set of recommendations pertains to the themes focused on *support* and *tenure/promotion*. Authors called for solidarity among faculty of color to address challenges faced by all members, rather than one or two subgroups. Rather than solely focusing on themselves, authors generally discussed advocating for others as a response to their personal lived experiences as faculty of color in academia. Those who participated in mentoring experiences described the mentor–mentee relationship positively and attributed successful outcomes achieved as a result of these relationships. Some authors also noted possessing privilege in some capacity and expressed the importance of using that privilege to influence change at their respective institutions. They also recommended being strategic in their service efforts by serving on high-profile committees and using these venues to draw attention to issues. The intended readers of this text are faculty of color, administrators, and other faculty. The personal narratives provide valuable insight, confirming and adding to the literature base regarding the lived experiences of faculty of color navigating scholarship, teaching, and service at PWIs. In addition to bringing awareness of what faculty of color often face, we anticipate that readers will use this knowledge to make positive systemic change, considering the recommendations. Finally, we hope this text will encourage continuous conversations with the intent of increasing truly inclusive environments within the academy. Primarily, authors demonstrate boldness in choosing not to use a pseudonym, when given the opportunity. It is quite evident that even here their resilience, self-advocacy, and advocacy for others are at work.

Editor and Author Bios

EDITORS

Dr. Karen Harris Brown is associate director of the Virgin Islands University Center for Excellence in Developmental Disabilities and associate professor of education at the University of the Virgin Islands. Prior to her current role, Dr. Brown was a tenured associate professor of speech-language pathology at a predominantly White institution and served as director of that program for three and a half academic years. She is the first African American to achieve tenure in her former department and first speech-language pathology faculty member to achieve tenure in her former program. Her research interests include family-centered care, the impact of stigma and disability in the Caribbean, and professional efficacy.

Dr. Patricia Alvarez McHatton is professor and dean of the College of Education and P-16 Integration at the University of Texas Rio Grande Valley. Her research interests focus on preparing culturally responsive educators and the educational experiences of culturally and linguistically diverse youth and families.

Dr. Michelle Frazier Trotman Scott is an associate professor of special education at the University of West Georgia. Her research interests include the achievement gap, special education overrepresentation, gifted education underrepresentation, creating culturally responsive classrooms, and increasing family involvement.

AUTHORS

Dr. Sohyun An is an associate professor of social studies education. She received her B.S. and M.S. degrees in social studies education from Seoul National University in South Korea and Ph.D. degree in curriculum and instruction from the University of Wisconsin–Madison. Her teaching and research is informed by critical race theory, AsianCrit, social justice education, and global citizenship education.

Tristan L. Glenn is an assistant professor of special education in the Inclusive Education Department at Kennesaw State University. His research focuses on culturally responsive pedagogy and the preparation of teacher candidates to effectively respond to issues of diversity in the classroom.

Paula Guerra is an associate professor of mathematics education in the Bagwell College of Education at Kennesaw State University. Her research interests include teaching math for social justice, schooling of Latinos, and English language learners and mathematics education.

Dr. Michael Hester is executive director of Special Programs at the University of West Georgia. During his 20 years in higher education, he has been a faculty member, Honors College dean, and director of debate.

Dr. Jacqueline Johnson is a full professor at a predominantly White institution.

Hema Ramanathan is an associate professor in the College of Education, University of West Georgia. Her interests are instructional leadership, teachers' professional development, English as a second language, issues of diversity, and comparative education. She is currently authoring an English language series of textbooks for schools in India.

Michael D. Smith is an assistant professor in the Teaching & Learning Department at SUNY New Paltz. His research focuses on culturally responsive pedagogy and teacher education.

Dr. Ursula Thomas is the director of Field Experience and Assessment of Teacher Education at Georgia State University–Perimeter College. Her research agenda includes issues of cultural mediation and its effects on instructional choices, the power of teacher educator research on diversity in the classroom, views of social justice in the early childhood classroom, preservice teachers' disposition on professionalism, diversity in teacher preparation programs, and critical issues in STEM and instructional technology.